ENDORSEMENTS

"This book has the power to hasten the healing process of anyone who has suffered the loss of a loved one. Even the most skeptical reader's beliefs will be altered after reading the incredible journey that this author undergoes from a near-death encounter to the metamorphosis of his gift to communicate with the other side.

This book is a must read for parents, spouses, friends, relatives ... anyone who is in mourning. Through reading about Chris's own experiences and those of his clients, the message is loud and clear that even though losing a loved one is a traumatic, life-altering experience, the deceased are still very much present and aware of our suffering for them. Death is not closure but a continuation of their love for us."

—Catherine Bowman
Author of *Crystal Awareness*, *Crystal Ascension*,
Entities Among Us and *The Golden One*

"Chris has helped many victim families find a level of peace by passing on messages from their loved ones. He uses his amazing gift to help others in the most selfless way possible. Thank you, Chris!"

—Margaret Miller
National President, MADD Canada 2007–2010

"Open your mind and open your heart, and the rest will follow—this I have learned from Chris Stillar. In the past several years I have witnessed Chris at work with many victims who have lost loved ones in tragic circumstances. I am always amazed at the reassurance and peace people find by attending his workshops.

MADD Canada has always maintained the belief that people should find comfort from the sources with which they are most comfortable. Over the years I have witnessed so many of our members find comfort through Chris. At MADD Canada's National Candlelight Vigil of Hope and Remembrance, Chris has become an integral part of the healing journey for so many, and for that we are extremely grateful. Personal healing comes in many forms, and Chris has been blessed with a way to help so many.

It has truly been an honour for me to write this for someone I have such a great respect and admiration for. I cannot imagine how difficult it must be for Chris on occasion, but I have never seen him without a smile on his face because he truly gets it—that he is here to help you whenever you're ready."

—Louise Knox
Chapter Services Manager, MADD Canada

"Chris has a gift that changes lives; anyone who has lost a loved one will have pain eased after just one hour with Chris. He opens your mind, heart and world like no one else can. Whether you believe that our spirits live on or not, there's no doubt they do after a reading. Chris gives our lives, and the lives of those passed, special meaning. It's euphoric to know this, as well as comforting and priceless."

—Jayne Pritchard
A Channel, CTV News Anchor and Certified Holistic Nutritionist

PENNIES FROM

Heaven

Sue
I hope you continue
to reach out in your
own way to those
in spirit. You have
a strong connection

Chris

PENNIES FROM
Heaven

A Medium's Two Cents on Life and Death

CHRISTOPHER STILLAR

BALBOA
PRESS

A DIVISION OF HAY HOUSE

Balboa Press books may be ordered through booksellers or by contacting:

Balboa Press
A Division of Hay House
1663 Liberty Drive
Bloomington, IN 47403
www.balboapress.com
1-(877) 407-4847

Because of the dynamic nature of the Internet, any web addresses or links contained in this book may have changed since publication and may no longer be valid. The views expressed in this work are solely those of the author and do not necessarily reflect the views of the publisher, and the publisher hereby disclaims any responsibility for them.

The author of this book does not dispense medical advice or prescribe the use of any technique as a form of treatment for physical, emotional, or medical problems without the advice of a physician, either directly or indirectly. The intent of the author is only to offer information of a general nature to help you in your quest for emotional and spiritual well-being. In the event you use any of the information in this book for yourself, which is your constitutional right, the author and the publisher assume no responsibility for your actions.

Any people depicted in stock imagery provided by Thinkstock are models, and such images are being used for illustrative purposes only.
Certain stock imagery © Thinkstock.

ISBN: 978-1-4525-3637-8 (e)
ISBN: 978-1-4525-3636-1 (sc)
ISBN: 978-1-4525-3638-5 (hc)

Library of Congress Control Number: 2011911414

Printed in the United States of America

Balboa Press rev. date: 7/11/2011

This book is dedicated to my Earth Angels.

No brighter lights have touched my life here on earth than
my children: Spencer, MacKenzie, Shelby and Sydney.

I may not always show it or say it often enough, and for that I am truly
sorry, but I believe you know how special you are to me. To be given
the honour of being your dad is the greatest gift I could imagine.

Now that I am on the path to finding me, my wish for you is a lifetime of
discovering, creating and loving who you truly are. Be all you can be in
every moment, in any manner you choose, and happiness will await you.

CONTENTS

FOREWORD

It was a cold January afternoon in 2002 when I first met Chris Stillar. I reluctantly accompanied my mother to her first reading with Chris. Calling me a skeptic at that time with respect to mediumship would have been a complete understatement. I was in my last year of university and was convinced that if items could not be scientifically studied, measured or quantified in some way, then they could not be real or legitimate. Little did I know on January 14, 2002, that I was about to get schooled in a whole new area, with Chris as my teacher.

My mother was seeking closure or some kind of reprieve from the grief she has been feeling from the sudden loss of her eldest brother, Don, who was diagnosed with leukemia and lost his courageous battle in seven weeks. She had heard about Chris through a random cleaner who serviced her office a few weeks before. We arrived and were greeted by Chris, who asked us to sit down with some urgency because "someone had been waiting for us." I rolled my eyes at such a notion, and with crossed arms I unenthusiastically took my seat next to my mother. Our reading lasted approximately forty-five minutes to an hour, during which time I had my eyes opened to a whole new world of possibility. Our reading was filled with validation after validation of my uncle's continued presence around us. Specific, private instances were drawn upon to illustrate the legitimacy of Chris's messages to us. We discussed things my uncle did not know in this life—and definitely things a virtual stranger would *never* know about our family and me specifically. We received complete information as to who he was to us; we got his name, the circumstances surrounding his death, specific phrases and things my mother had said to him on his death bed when he was in a comatose state to confirm he heard every word. Chris even drew out his hairline and moustache with his hands to let us know he had gotten all his hair back, which was lost during intense chemotherapy. My uncle was not the only one to visit us that day and provide such detailed, specific validations.

I sat astonished and was brought to tears when faced first with the knowledge that my uncle was really still with us, just in another form, and second by the humbling fact that I was so narrow-minded and unevolved that, until that moment, I refused to believe in what was unfolding before me. Attending this reading was akin to opening a Pandora's Box of emotions, thoughts and questions for me. When the reading concluded, it was as if Chris had given my mother a million dollars. I have never seen her so uplifted and instantly changed. It was almost four weeks to the day that complications from leukemia had taken my uncle from his physical body, but today was the day my mother's grief for him ceased to exist. My spirituality and belief system were forever changed that day as well.

Chris Stillar undeniably has a gift. It is not something that can be scientifically measured or quantified but only felt to be confirmed, like love. His purpose is not to provide lottery numbers, give advice or be a conduit (like in the film *Ghost*). He provides a place where one can come for conversations with a loved one who has crossed over. He is there to provide validations that the people who have passed are still around you. It is not a guaranteed resolution to grief, but it can be. It can also be a great point to start healing. Beyond this purpose it is a great place to open your mind to the possibility that there is something more happening then we are physically aware of. You can start to remove your egocentric ideas that we as physical bodies are the only things that inhabit our physical space. It could be received as a test to your faith and belief system, no matter what the depth and nature of it. I am not a religious person, and I don't believe in or subscribe to organized religion in *any* form for more reasons than I wish to state here. However I am a spiritual person who now believes that there is something beyond this physical life we lead, that we are not alone, and when our loved ones leave us, they don't really—they just change their form.

Since my initial meeting with Chris, I have seen him alone on a few occasions, and so have several members of my extended family, circle of friends and acquaintances, including my husband all the way from California. They have similar experiences to mine in the sense that the validations were accurate, specific and personal. Not one person I know has ever had a remotely negative experience with Chris and his abilities. Each person took away unique experiences and lessons from his or her time with Chris. I am proud to know someone who, by his faith and dedication to helping others, has been able to share his gift and reach so many lives. The content of this book is his truth, not intended to sell you on anything or convince you to make it yours. From my perspective it is a true account of his experiences, thoughts, feelings and philosophies that are intended to be shared, perhaps received as a learning tool and as inspiration.

But don't take it from me. This phenomenon must be experienced and felt in order to be accepted and truly comprehended. Reading this book is the first step and will reinforce what I just shared. Even if the only validation you receive is that your mind is open to possibility, it is a wonderful place to start in your personal evolution. Skepticism in life is a very healthy way to approach new experiences, and it certainly enhances them, especially if the outcome is the polar opposite of what you expect or initially believe. Expectations also play a role in what you take from an experience such as this, so release them. Expect to have an experience and let anything beyond that become an additional gift.

Chris Stillar has been a healer, a teacher, an inspiration and now a friend. I'm pleased that he has this medium, the printed page, to be able to inspire you to open your minds and hearts to the energy, spirits and possibilities that surround you.

Lisa Graystone
Writer and Fashion Entrepreneur, Owner of Evolution Vintage

PREFACE

So much is awaiting us; we just need to take the first step in creating who and what we will be at any given moment. If we believe that great things happen by circumstance or coincidence, this might be the perfect time to evaluate our belief systems. We create our realities day in and day out. The camouflage of life has most people believing in fate or coincidence, but don't be fooled. It is time to take control of our lives and never give it away again. Declare ownership of both the good and the not so good. Once you realize you are in control of your destiny and are the "soul" creator of your future, the possibilities are endless.

Many people find it easier to believe life or God has thrown them a curve ball. They tend to blame anyone or anything, thus giving their power away. How many people say, "What else could I expect," or perhaps, "My luck is so bad; I knew it was just a matter of time before something like this happened"? These statements are examples of people giving away their power. They act as if they have no say in or control over the unfolding of their lives. It is true that some things happen to us that we haven't consciously chosen, and although we may have no control over the situation, we always have control over how we react to it. There are always several options from which to choose. If something has happened to you, or you have done something that you know is not a true reflection of who you are, change your thoughts about it and act differently.

Stop giving the power away and take ownership of your life. When we don't take responsibility for all the circumstances of our lives, we eliminate any possibility for change. We perceive of ourselves as victims and give away the internal strength necessary for change. I do not believe there are any victims.

My life has always had purpose, but I was unaware of what that was until I opened myself to the world of spirit. This momentous event was an epiphany, a shedding of the old me, a walk through a doorway into a new, vibrant world of truth, beauty and simplicity, compelling me to write my story, my version of truth and who I am. This book is written not only to help others who walk the path of self-discovery, but to validate our beliefs and feelings about life and to offer assurances that unconditional love is available to each and every one of us.

Although at times I may be confused as to my life's direction, I realize my path is clearly marked. I have two trusted friends with me at all times. Grey Owl and Gabriel are always by my side, Gabriel on my left and Grey Owl on my right. Not only do I feel their presence, but I see them. They are my spirit guides, ever present, ever loving and non-judgmental.

The writing of this book was inspired by—and, in part, made possible by—two very special people, each of whom have touched my life in a dramatic and loving fashion: my grandmother, Bessie (now in the spirit world and someone I will talk more about later), and a dear, distant friend I had the pleasure of meeting only five times named Rosemary Altea, who profoundly touched my life through her book *Eagle and the Rose*. Rosemary became a beacon of light to me with her life-altering advice.

Although in 1966 I opened my eyes for the first time to this wondrous world, I never truly saw it until three decades later. For close to thirty years I went through life as if sleepwalking, barely functioning. I did the minimum to ensure my physical and emotional survival without any attempt to enhance my spiritual side. Only now, when I see more clearly, am I able to understand the meaning of my life.

My story is your story and your story is my story, because we are all one with God. I invite you to sit back, read my truth and create your own. Whenever possible, the actual names are used in the telling of these remarkable true life accounts of spirit communication. For the protection of my clients, some names have been changed to maintain their anonymity. Thank you for choosing to be a part of this process!

Chris Stillar

ACKNOWLEDGMENTS

This book has been both a labour of love and a lesson in frustration and hard work. In truth, I would not have it any other way. My name may appear on this book alone, but please understand that countless and many nameless people have contributed to it over my forty-four-plus years of life.

To all of those wonderful people who are mentioned in *Pennies from Heaven* and have allowed their stories to be told, all in an attempt to bring healing and help to others, I thank you.

Thanks to MADD Canada, for your continued support and friendship over the past several years. It has been an honour for me to work with you and your families.

To Catherine Haller and Catherine Bowman for your editing skills, generosity in time and genuine interest in my book; thank you.

To my lifetime and unconditional friends: Lynda Lovett, Margrit Wolley, Marlene Callaghan and Gary and Denise Heaslip. Know your friendships are true treasures to me, and your unwavering support for me and my work has inspired me when perhaps I had lost belief in myself. I cherish these friendships beyond description; simply I say thank you!

To my family—Mom, Dad, Tracey, Mike, Camryn and Riley—I am blessed beyond measure to have your love and support. Thank you.

To my best friend and wife, Kim. I have learned that with you anything is possible; thank you for loving me and seeing through my imperfections.

To my four children, Spencer, MacKenzie, Shelby and Sydney. When you were little, I always said you were gifts from God; please know no truer words will be written in this book. Thank you for teaching me far more than I could ever teach you.

To those bright lights of energy and love; better known as spirits who have trusted me for the last fifteen years to convey their messages to their loved ones, I thank you all for the trust, teaching and inspiration you have brought to my life by helping me live a life of purpose and joy. I have always felt blessed to share your thoughts, feelings and emotions to those who struggle to see, hear, feel and perhaps believe in your presence.

To my group of guides, better known as Grey Owl, Gabriel and my Unsung Heroes: you know how much I value our friendship and your guidance in my life and work. Thank you.

Last, but certainly not least, to God: I have always believed in you, I have always known you existed and I give thanks for experiencing you and for knowing you as a friend.

PART 1

Chapter 1
METAMORPHOSIS

Nowhere to turn. A feeling of hopelessness surrounds me, and my days of wandering in a cloud of uncertainty are about to end. Self-destruction is all that runs through my head. The pain—oh, the pain—it must be stopped. I walk through the kitchen and into the living room, unsure of my next step. Turning to my left, I begin to climb the stairs. Step after step, I take what will be my final walk. I clutch the railing for support as I struggle to make my way to the top. Pausing but for a second, I reconsider what I know will come next.

I'm in a dark tunnel, and all I can see is straight ahead of me. Life has stopped; my actions are not happening in real time. What is real time? I know that I am not myself. Everything is surreal and dreamlike. I turn left and enter my bedroom. I close the door behind me. The house is so quiet. There are no sounds except those in my head. I walk over to my bed and sit down on the edge. Sunlight is streaming through the window to my left; the warmth encompasses me. Dust particles dance across the beams of light, but all I see is darkness. The rays of the sun fall on my tired body, but nothing can save me. I am consumed with only myself.

As I sit there, I think about those who have accused me of this awful crime. I know in my heart that I did not hurt that little girl. I loved her and could never hurt her.

This is my only option because no one will ever believe the truth. I reach down, and from under the bed I pull up my rifle. I sit for what seems an eternity, and then my decision is made. I raise the rifle, turning the barrel toward my head. I bring it closer and closer to my face. Finally it rests against my skin. The sharp, cold metal of the barrel feels cool as it brushes against my flesh. The echoing in my head becomes louder, and then all goes still.

I pull the trigger***!

Suddenly I see a body slumped forward on the bed. It's no longer me that I'm viewing. Instead, I sense myself standing in the corner closest to the door that I walked through just moments before, and I am watching this poor man bleeding, but he is absent from all physical pain. One moment I was this man struggling for answers—I felt his pain and sensed his total despair—and the next moment I am watching the aftermath of his choice play out in front of me, a silent observer.

Everything goes quiet, and I find myself back in my office. Never before has anyone from spirit walked me through his or her actual death. The clarity and the reality of this are so overwhelming that it takes me a few moments before I can comprehend the magnitude of what has taken place. I witnessed this man's final act, but more than that, I *was* this man for a few brief moments in time. I felt what he felt; I thought what he thought. I am confused. Moments pass as I attempt to gather my composure. My client, Sam, who sits across from me, is filled with emotions; she desperately fights to hold back her tears. Finally, she speaks.

"That was my uncle. You accurately described the way he was found. You even described the house. How is that possible?"

"I'm not completely sure how it works, but I know your uncle found it important enough to come through to explain to you what was happening to him at that time. He makes reference to a woman and a young girl. The reason for his suicide is based around these two people. What I can't tell you is why he needs you to know these things," I answered.

"I do," she said, in relief. "There have always been rumours within our family that it was not suicide. There has been talk that someone besides my uncle was involved in his death."

"Sam, you can rest assured that his death was a result of his own actions."

"Thank you."

Sam's family story is just one of many I have been privy to. You see, I am a *medium*. I have an ability that enables me to help people. We all have talents and the ability to help others; the question is whether we choose to use them or not. As a medium, I use my ability to help those here in the physical realm as well as those who live in spirit.

I have discovered, without question, that we continue on after physical death. Death is nothing more than a change in energy; we shed our heavy earthly bodies. At the time of death, we consciously live from our souls. We reside in our souls, even while in the physical world before death, but we are simply unaware of this. If you believe that your body only defines who you are, you are mistaken. I do not have all the answers, and I realize that this is only my truth. It rings of beauty, love and peace for me. What is your truth? No matter what one's truth is, if it is authentic, it will bring you comfort.

The Change ...

When I discovered my gift of mediumship, I was twenty-nine years old, at least ninety pounds overweight and unhappy with my life. Nothing I did or achieved had made me truly happy. But from March 4, 1996, to August 16, 1996, my life's path had been vastly altered by a series of personal and financial events. The timing of these events caused me to take a good look at how I was living my life. I could no longer skip from job to job or crisis to crisis; my days of running away were over. It wasn't until sufficient time had passed and the dust had settled that I could look back and see how these incidents were actual blessings and not God playing a cruel game with my life. I had turned a corner, and there was no going back.

Once I began to look honestly at life, God and how I had merely been sleepwalking in the past, I was able to make better choices to help create the "me" I wanted to be. I looked closer at past choices and the repetitious habits that I played out over and over. I developed the desire to read, devouring one book after another. Until this point, I had read only three books: one I chose to read and two others were required for school. Reading was a torture I did not want to experience; it was easier to turn on the television than to pick up a book.

Once my enthusiasm for spirit communication, God and spirituality had been unleashed, I could not read enough. Not only was I reading, but I was beginning to understand how the books helped me see myself honestly. I could see how the truth in the pages spilled over into my life. Books served as a mirror that enabled me to view my life head-on. Even though I remained extremely skeptical about a lot of things, much of what I read resonated deep within me. I made a conscious decision to change various aspects of my life.

The first change involved my eating habits. I had always known that a thinner person inside was trying to get out, although for the most part I was not unhappy about being obese. I had been heavy all my life, and it was all I knew. One day, following a personal tragedy, I decided I had had enough. I wanted to make a change—I needed to make a change—and the transition began, not just physically but psychologically and spiritually as well. I was changing completely. Those series of events in 1996 were the catalysts I needed in order to see clearly. Although they didn't actually change my essence, I remained the same "me," the same soul, and these circumstances helped to show me that the "who" I was portraying myself as was not the "who" I wanted to be any longer. I finally realized that the ball had always been in my court. I always had the ability to change who I was to who I wanted to be, and I took charge of my life for the first time.

My physical image changed, and my beliefs became clearer and stronger. I could now look back on my life and past events and see beauty and perfection where once I saw nothing but ugliness, regret and self-pity.

As the excess weight started to come off, I left behind some aspects of myself that were no longer required. People around me noticed the changes, and some realized it was more than just physical change. Not everyone was comfortable with how I now presented myself. Family members worried about me. Those that knew me always thought I had a great sense of humour, but suddenly they could no longer sense it.

People often tell me that I am a lucky person. Everything I want seems to come easily for me. Although I believe I am blessed, not everything has been easy. Life has held many events and surprises for me, and some are still to come. The difference now is how I choose to view these events. Instead of being a passive recipient and believing that the good and bad just occur beyond my control, I now know that I bring everything to me. Everything that we would deem good, bad and mundane is a result of our own actions and choices. I understand that there are no coincidences, luck (good or bad) or lives destined to fate. All we have is life based on personal choice. Every action, thought and deed has a reaction.

Unlike Sam's uncle, I felt I had many avenues to explore, new worlds to discover and a sense of purpose to guide me into the next chapter of my life. I can't help but see the change in my life, my metamorphosis if you will, as a comparison to a caterpillar transitioning into a butterfly. For far too many years, I had cocooned myself and my life, only to feel like I had broken free of a binding and restrictive existence to take flight like a grand monarch discovering a whole new world for the first time.

Chapter 2
MY JOURNEY BEGINS

Although I am often asked how and when I became a medium, I'm not certain there is a simple answer. In June 1994, I was just starting my day at the newspaper office where I worked. Earlier that morning the regulars had met for coffee at the local coffee shop. I left feeling somewhat lightheaded and unable to focus my thoughts on any one area. I tried to start my daily agenda but felt lost. I got up and walked next door to a client's store to talk to her, hoping that this strange feeling would pass. It did not. During that short visit I could not hold a conversation, and at one point I could not even remember the person's name, even though I had worked with her for the last five years. I was not the least bit worried about what was happening to me, but I was irritated that I could not remember the names of my friends and co-workers.

When my editor came back from coffee, I asked him to drive me to the hospital, where I went to my wife's office to tell her something was very wrong. I remember being taken to the emergency department. I know I took off my shirt, and the last thing I remember is leaning over the sink, sick to my stomach. I woke up approximately fifteen hours later, at about two in the morning, to see my mother and my Aunt Elaine standing at the foot of my bed. Mom seemed relieved I was conscious and started asking me what I considered to be extremely stupid questions. "Do you know who we are? Do you know where you are?" I answered her questions appropriately, although I had no idea what had transpired.

I soon found out I had completely faded from reality the day before and didn't recognize my wife nor any of my family. The doctors did test after test to find out what was wrong. They did drug screens, sent me to a bigger city hospital in an ambulance for a CAT scan and performed a lumbar puncture. They didn't detect any aneurysms, no drugs showed up and nothing was produced from the spinal tap. The doctors were baffled, and my family was extremely worried. As strangely as it began, I started to come out of it. I was in the hospital for two days and then was permitted to go home for a few days of bed rest. Anyone who has ever been through a spinal tap knows that it is best to lie flat on your back for about three days afterward. I do not remember if those instructions had been spelled out to me, but if they were, I didn't listen. I was up and down too much and paid the price for it. The headaches came on fast and furious, more severe than anything I had ever experienced before. The worst one caused me to grab hold of the vanity with one hand and the back of my head with the other while a horrendous pain ripped through my head. I felt as if the back portion of my skull had exploded. I remember reaching back expecting to feel a gaping hole. I screamed for my wife, and she came running. I still do not know what took place in my brain stem that evening, but I believe whatever happened was the beginning of a physical change in my brain that now enables me to make contact with those in spirit.

The attending physician who was working the emergency department that day had done all the appropriate tests and could not determine what had happened. This did not sit well with my father, so he managed to get me in to see a specialist at Wellesley Hospital in Toronto. The doctor looked at the records, examined me and hooked me up to more wires. Lastly an EEG was done. When the doctor consulted with me, he could not explain the cause; the best he could say was that it may or may not happen again. I felt the whole episode was stress related, so about one month later I quit my stressful job without having another to go to.

I cannot say with certainty whether the illness had anything to do with my ability to communicate with those in the spirit world, but two years later I had another turning point. The events of August 1996 had a very profound effect on me.

Grandma

My grandmother, Bessie, had been suffering from breathing problems that seemed to come and go. At times it was hard for us to detect because Grandma never complained, but now it happened more frequently and was taking its toll on this vital lady. My family and I were with her and my aunt on the long weekend in August when she asked to visit the cemetery. I took her as we stood over Grandpa's grave looking at the headstone. Grandma turned to me, pointed and said, "I guess I will be laid on this side."

I looked at her and said, "Not in the near future; I know you'll be here for a long time yet." The rest of the visit was incredible, and I remember as we backed out of her driveway and waved good-bye, that even though I could not consciously admit it, I was visiting her for the last time.

Within days she was rushed to the hospital with an attack of angina. Her heart surgery was scheduled three days later. The evening before the surgery, I called Grandma to tell her that everything would be fine. I said I loved her and would see her the following weekend. Her last words to me were, "I love you and will see you sometime."

A lump formed in my throat as I said good-bye. Her surgery started at 7:45 a.m. and was scheduled to last until 1:00 p.m. I was on the phone back and forth all day with my aunt, and there was no word. At 3:30 p.m. my father called me on his way home from work and told me they had run into complications, and it didn't look good for her. He was leaving for Sudbury immediately. I hung up the phone, made the necessary arrangements and set off with my wife, our eight month old baby and my sister for Sudbury.

It was the longest drive I have ever made; the four hours seemed much longer. I prayed all the way up even though I knew the outcome. We reached the hospital at 8:45 p.m. and were met by my father, my aunt and my uncle. Dad had just arrived and had not been up to the surgical floor yet. Just then my uncle's wife came running down crying, saying it didn't look good and that we should go up and speak with the nurse. The elevator doors opened. and there were my two aunts. Because both were crying, I was certain Grandma had died. We were told about an hour later that the doctor wanted to speak to us, so the floor nurse led us to the hospital chapel. Now we knew. Only half of our family was there when the doctor came in. "It was tough," the doctor said. Before he could say anything else, my father stood up shook his hand and thanked him for all that he had done for his mother. The doctor said, "She's still with us, but we thought we had lost her around supper time."

I will never forget the expression on my aunt's face as her eyes lit up and a smile crossed her face. She said, "Thank you, God." Now we had hope. The doctor stated that the next forty-eight hours would be crucial. He also said that she had been on the heart-lung bypass unit much longer than normal, and her operation, which should have taken five hours, had turned into twelve. He also told us that she needed to wake up within the next twenty-four hours.

We were elated, and even though I felt that God had answered our prayers, I did not stop praying. When we were allowed to see her in the critical care unit two at a time, I had no idea what to expect and felt ill. She lay there with more tubes and wires running into her than I could have imagined. A large cotton bandage covered her open chest. There was little resemblance to the woman that waved good-bye to me just one week earlier. I bent over, kissed her forehead and told her I loved her.

For the entire night and the next day, I walked, sat, cried and prayed. I prayed harder than I had ever prayed before for a miracle. My countless trips to the altar brought me much-needed peace until it eventually dawned on me that we had to accept not only the fact that Grandma may go, but that it may be what was best for her. On Friday morning at 2:00 a.m., I was sleeping for the first time in two days when my uncle knocked on the hotel room door and said we had to get to the hospital fast. When we arrived, the nurse led us to Grandma's bedside. We crowded into her room, taking turns telling her we loved her and that it was okay for her to go home now. We kissed her and rubbed her hands, and then as the numbers on the life support machine started to drop, I backed out of the room. The nurse stood next to me, and I said, "She's already gone hasn't she?" The nurse looked at me and nodded. As I walked down the corridor with my aunt I hugged her and said, "Acceptance sucks."

Within an hour we had packed up and were driving home to get clothes for the funeral. Back in my grandmother's house, while writing her eulogy, I realized we had in fact received a miracle that weekend. The day she died, two of my cousins were involved in a very serious car accident in Toronto. While they were at a gas station waiting for the vehicle in front to pull away from the pump, a large dump truck lost control and rammed into them. The impact sent their vehicle flying past the first gas pump, missing it only by inches, and through the building's front wall. The car was destroyed, but my cousins received only minor injuries. They were badly bruised and suffered from severe stiffness and pain for quite some time, but as one police officer had said, they were very lucky to be alive. Our family could easily have lost three people within a matter of hours. The miracle we prayed for was not the one we needed at the time. My grandmother's life had been completed, but my cousins had many more years to fulfill their mission. Once again I gave thanks to God.

The next two days were very hard. I stood up at her funeral, looked out at the congregation and was astounded at the number of people in attendance. The balcony was full, a partition had been removed to enlarge the main seating area and the sound system was on in the basement for those who couldn't find room upstairs. Grandma wouldn't have had it any other way. Even in death she got what she wanted, a full house. As I started to read the eulogy I had written, I felt calm and peaceful knowing that I was not only talking to those in attendance but also to Grandma. At that time, I had no idea how the loss of that special person was going to affect me; if I had, I certainly would not have believed it.

My Journey Is Underway

The Friday following my grandmother's death, I was at home with my three children. They had just finished watching one of their preschool shows, and I was flipping through the channels. When I saw Maury Povich I stopped. I was seldom home during the weekday, and his talk show was not something I normally watched. It is obvious to me now why I turned to that show, but at the time I had no idea what was awaiting me. Until that day I doubt I had ever heard the word "medium." I was mesmerised by Maury's guest, Rosemary Altea, who was describing to two women how their sons had committed suicide. Although I am normally a skeptical person, something powerful gripped me that day. By the end of the show, when they were promoting Rosemary's first book, *The Eagle and the Rose*, I called the local bookstore to have one set aside for me. Then I bundled up my children, loaded them into my car and headed down the highway in the pouring rain to pick it up. Later that day I began to read the book that would alter my life.

After reading *The Eagle and the Rose*, I was hooked on Rosemary's story and wanted to know more about this phenomenon called mediumship. I certainly didn't think I would become a medium, but if I was ever able to communicate with spirits, helping people would be very important to me.

Rosemary's work guided me to other books on how to meet one's spirit guides, mediumship and channeling. I finally tried to seriously meditate for the first time. As I sat quietly in my office, focusing on my chakras to still myself, lights danced across my closed eyes and provided a spectrum of colour and movement.

After a few moments, I sensed someone standing behind me. This strange, new presence brought comfort and warmth. The occurrence inspired me to meditate at least once a day to try to discover who this being was. Finally after several attempts, a voice so clear and strong said to me, "I am Grey Owl."

Over the next few days, as I continued to meditate I felt this strong presence standing about a foot behind me on my right side. I sensed a quiet man with a strong presence. It wasn't until after a couple of weeks that I finally had some communication in the form of one or two words accompanied by a symbol shown to me in my head. What I heard or saw would be a word such as dog, teapot or maybe a picture of a house, all in an attempt to bring a message across to me. Complete sentences did not arrive for at least a month.

The more contact I made with Grey Owl, the more I learned about myself and my new friend. I knew instinctively that not only was he my spirit guide, but that he was always with me and had been since the day I was born. My trust for Grey Owl grew in leaps and bounds. I learned that what I considered coincidence in the past was my silent friend working hard to make the pieces of my life fall into place. Even when the pieces did not seem to fit, or when harsh lessons seemed to fall upon me, they were well-timed pieces of a puzzle that was beginning to come together.

I had never found anything in my life about which I was passionate. I would sink my teeth into a new venture, but as soon as it began, I lost interest and it ended. This was different; this was a comfort level I had never experienced before, something that I knew I was destined to experience. I couldn't wait. One month ago I wasn't even aware mediumship was a legitimate ability, and now I was beginning to develop this talent for myself. When a baby duck swam for the first time, the ability came naturally, and so it was with my birth into mediumship. A month passed with my being able to make contact with Grey Owl every day or two.

I asked Grey Owl about his life. He informed me that he had lived on earth as a part Ojibwa and part Cree Indian. His answers excited me because for the first time I was getting information that I hoped I could verify. When I questioned Grey Owl as to where he had lived, the answer was crystal clear: Montana. He went on to say he had died in 1847. As I probed as to where and how his death occurred, without warning, I found myself standing next to Grey Owl on a tall rock face that overlooked a raging river. As I watched him standing in full strength and glory, I sensed the respect he had for this sacred land. When I looked down from the top of the rock face, I could see the river split in two and flow in different directions. He explained that he lost his footing and slipped to his death from the very spot we were standing, but he quickly explained that he never hit the ground. He told me he literally flew out of his body, and his soul took flight and soared over the tops of the pines. When I asked about any family and friends left behind, he simply stood silently with arms folded. Again I repeated the question, and again he did not reply. To this day Grey Owl has not found the need to talk more about his personal life, and I have lost the need to ask.

When my trip into Grey Owl's past was complete, I knew I had to verify what had been told to me, but I was uncertain where to start. I called the local library and asked if they had any books regarding North American Natives. I knew that the Ojibwa were native to my home province of Ontario, Canada, but I had no idea where the Cree had lived. The librarian said there was an atlas that showed the areas where each nation lived, and although this particular reference guide could not be signed out, she would be happy to get it and try to answer any questions I had. I told her I was interested in the 1847 period and asked if the Ojibwa and Cree had lived in the state of Montana. I was ready to be disappointed, but she said yes, they had both lived in parts of that state. I thanked her and hung up. There was my proof, all the verification I needed. At this point I needed proof, because I did not as yet trust what was happening to me. The knowledge that this was real gave me such a natural high that I walked around for days in a state of euphoria.

Gabriel Comes into My Life

During another meditation in November 1996, a second presence joined Grey Owl and me. This new energy stood behind my left shoulder and a little to the side. It felt like a young adult male, and upon asking for his name, I heard, "Gabriel." I immediately questioned whether I just picked out a name that I liked, or whether the spirit had actually told me his name. It has been over fourteen years since that day, and he is still with me. It wasn't until six months later that I discovered this guide shared the same name as an archangel. I do not know whether they are one and the same because Gabriel has never divulged his past. I know that when I see him, he is dressed in white robes, and his hair is sandy blond, short and curly. I know that he is here to help with my mediumship and gives me so much support and encouragement, and that I am a better person because of our friendship. I am thankful he is with me.

When I'm feeling sorry for myself, Gabriel and Grey Owl never hesitate to tell me that this behaviour does nothing to serve who I truly am. When I am ready to carry on, so are my friends. They do not criticize or judge; they simply point out what is so obvious that it is a wonder I missed it. I thank them and tell them I love them. God is a perfect energy, and my two guides are wonderful examples of how God operates.

Within three short months in 1996, I had gone from leading what I thought was a run-of-the-mill lifestyle to being a full-blown spiritual medium with a host of spirits ready willing and able to guide not only my life, but my friends and acquaintances as well. My journey had begun.

Chapter 3
MY LIFE THE MOSAIC

As a young child, I enjoyed a typical family life with its share of dysfunction. I grew up 60 miles north of Toronto in the small, picturesque village of Everett, a community of about 360 nestled in a valley surrounded by two rivers and miles of lush farmland.

I remember being curious about God, death and the purpose of life as a little boy—pretty heavy needs for a child of six or seven. At the same time I wanted answers, I was also scared of death, God and the unknown. What little I knew about God came from Grandmother Bessie, a staunch Christian who went to church twice a week and read the Bible daily. She was a warm-hearted woman who loved her family and God. I loved my visits to Port Loring, my grandmother's hometown. I considered it my second home, and when it came time to return to Everett after a weekend or summer vacation, I would sit in the backseat of the car crying my eyes out. Oh, how I loved that place and her!

During those childhood visits, my grandmother made sure I went to Sunday school. This was my entire contact with organized religion, and for me, it was enough. Religion is good for some people, but it wasn't for me. It only created more unanswered questions. I know now that was a good thing.

This writing is not intended as religion bashing; I simply want to point out why it wasn't right for me. I have always believed in God, although I never knew who God was or what that meant. To this day I continue to learn about God, and for that I give thanks. As a child and a sinner, I was scared. Being a "sinner" at six was not a great start to life. I thought God punished us for our mistakes, loved us when we were good and judged us when we were bad. This concept stayed with me for years, yet I knew in my heart, my soul, my very essence that it was not true. It was so hard to go against everything one had been taught, especially when the teachings were based in fear.

At the tender age of eight and a half, I lost my standing as an only child. Along came my one and only sibling, and my parents named her Tracey. To sum her up, I would say she was one who always smiled, and she was a girl with a big heart who could get on my nerves faster than anyone. The age difference certainly didn't help matters.

My parents are Clint and Linda Stillar, incredible parents who were not perfect but did the best they could, and I thank them not only for all they have done but also for all they did not do for me. Upon Tracey's arrival, my room was moved downstairs in our family home. This was likely one of the reasons I had issues with Tracey throughout my childhood. Our house was a new bungalow that my father built. Although the basement was fully finished and furnished, it was still a basement and, in my eyes, a hell; I was terrified to sleep in alone. Not only did my mind play tricks on me, but my eyes viewed images that horrified me.

I was not beaten as a child, and my family did not abuse me in any way, but sleeping in the basement was my own personal nightmare. I would lie awake with the blankets pulled up to my neck, all my extremities tucked safely inside and my eyes glued to the open bedroom door. The hall light stayed on all night while my mind worked overtime. I would wait, knowing for sure that some dark, grey figure would slide up the hallway, enter my room and get me. Each night after my parents were asleep, I would grab my pillow and blankets and head up to the main floor of the house.

My trip up the stairs should have been quick and painless, but I was not that fortunate. My nightly climb involved moments of sheer terror as I slowly ascended from my dungeon of horror. With every step I turned my head back and stared down the empty hallway, sure that my next step would be my last. I knew the devil himself would spring out and take me away. Nearly frozen with fear, I would continue my climb until finally I reached the safety of the main floor and made my way to my parents' room. I don't know how many months or years I slept on the floor or in the bed next to Mom and Dad. At times I still think I might have been the cause of my parents' divorce. Three sharing a bedroom did not help a marriage. Sometimes I even slept with my baby sister. Isn't it funny how a child's mind works? I thought a one-year-old could save me from the evil that lurked in my basement.

Finally the time came when I could sleep in my own bed all night long. The hall light stayed on and my door remained open, but at least I stayed in my room. Then the nightmares started coming on a regular basis. I can look back and laugh when I talk about it now, and I can even understand why it began. I am and always have been a smart ass, one of the class clowns. My sense of humour has worked for me all through my life. As an overweight child I didn't think I had a lot going for me, but I loved to laugh and to make others laugh. I never shied away from being the centre of attention; most of the time I craved it. It was all there in my nightmare: Slowly I stepped out of my bed and walked cautiously toward my bedroom door. Then, holding my breath, I would make a mad dash for the stairs. One, two, three stairs, and finally I was more than halfway up, standing on the landing, and nothing was coming after me. There were only four stairs left and nothing bad in sight. As I resumed my climb, I turned and called the demon that wasn't in sight an asshole. Without missing a beat, this black figure would dart out of the furnace room and up the stairs to grab me by the leg and start pulling me back down, ripping at my flesh. I would bolt up in a terror-stricken panic.

I don't know how many times I had this dream, but it played itself out over at least two years. Sometimes I would get to the very last step before turning around and yelling some pathetic curse word at the demon, but every time he would get me. Never did that demon come for me until I opened my mouth to taunt him. I guess I was slow to catch on, and depending who you asked today, people would probably say not much has changed. Keep your mouth shut and all will be well—a pretty simple motto to live by, but not for me. I think this was an attempt by my subconscious to teach me a simple rule of life. I preferred to learn things the hard way.

Discovering God

As a child I felt I was different—not better, but different from the other kids. I knew that great things were waiting for me; what they were I didn't know, and I still don't. I just knew I was special, because we are all special in our own ways and in the eyes of God. I believe that what I was experiencing was my first realization of faith—faith in God, faith in myself and faith in life. There was an undeniable comfort in knowing all would be fine.

One night I was in my downstairs bedroom suffering from a most incredible pain in my midsection. I was about ten years old and had been experiencing these pains for quite some time. My parents had taken me to the family doctor, and I had been examined but had no recollection of the course of treatment, if any. I remember lying there crying because the pain was so intense. Looking back, I can see a scared little boy lying in his bed. Then this little boy did something different: he started praying to God for help. I don't know how long I prayed, but I know I didn't stop until the pain went away. When the pain left, it was instantaneous. The tears stopped, and I opened my eyes and saw a wondrous sight above my bed, just below the ceiling. There directly above me was a large hand opened with its palm down. I could hardly believe what I was seeing. I thanked God, and from that moment on I knew without a doubt that God existed and that He loved me. I had always believed in God, but the difference that night was that I experienced God.

Looking Back

No matter how clear we think our memories are, we can be sure that time has altered our perception of events. We forget facts or insert adjectives to enhance the story and even change the details. For the most part this is not done deliberately and occurs because time has elapsed. The more time between the incident and the memory, the greater the alterations.

Keeping this in mind, I will try to describe certain events in my life. Special attention has been paid throughout the book to the truth, and I believe I have not purposely embellished events to make them read better. While you read this book, or for that matter any book, remain in touch with your true feelings about what you are reading. Look inside yourself for the answers to whether or not what you are reading is true for you.

The following accounts include my fascination with Native North Americans and my fears, as a child, of séances, graveyards and Ouija boards. They remain as testaments to who I am and where I come from.

In remembering my childhood, I see different events that have lead me to where I am today. At the time these experiences were nothing but a child's life unfolding, and I never gave them a second thought. As a child I had an overwhelming fascination with Native North Americans. I could not get enough of Westerns on television, but not the standard Westerns; they had to be movies that featured Indians, and regardless of the situation, I always rooted for the natives. Even then I cheered for the underdog. I knew how the movies would end, with the natives never winning a fight, but that didn't stop me from hoping they would.

I know that I drove my parents crazy with my obsession. I had to have the feathered headdress, vest, moccasins, drum and tomahawk. It didn't end there. On many days one would find me as a five-year-old running around my grandmother's house with only a string tied around my waist and toilet paper hanging down the front and back. It wasn't the best loincloth invention, but it served its purpose. On every trip up north, regardless of the time of day or night, I always insisted on seeing the tepee that was erected outside a trading post on the side of Highway 11, just south of Burk's Falls. If I was asleep late at night, without fail my parents would reach back to the seat where I was curled up and nudge me. It wasn't until they said the tent was coming up that I would sit straight up and gaze out the window. Once we passed the wooden tepee I would collapse back down and return to sleep. All was wonderful in my world.

But it was more than an obsession; I truly believed I was an Indian. A relative once told me that my great grandmother was part Indian. It wasn't until I was thirty-four years old that I discovered that she was actually of German descent.

I don't know if I was a native Indian in a past life or if this obsession was my connection to Grey Owl. It makes sense to me now, and I understand how Grey Owl's presence was friendly and nonthreatening when I first became aware of him.

As a young child I was also fascinated by certain television shows, and I watched them faithfully every week. I would get caught up in the make-believe of *The Six Million Dollar Man*, *The Bionic Woman*, *Bewitched*, *Wonder Woman* and *The Man from Atlantis*. I totally bought into bionics, witchcraft and even a man who lived underwater. I whole-heartedly believed in the magic. I would run around the house jumping off beds and leaping over things and pretending I had bionic legs, or I would sit and practice twitching my nose in order to move an object.

Other childhood events that I recall with clarity are the times my parents went out for the evening, and two local teenage girls came to babysit. I was no more than six or seven, and these two girls would bring over a couple of friends. We would head for the basement and sit in a circle on the floor with just a glimmer of light coming through the doorway from upstairs, and they would try to summon the dead. In fear and silence we sat holding hands, and then Helen or Cathy would ask for the spirits of Jack the Ripper or Janis Joplin to come in. As a six-year-old I had never heard of these people. My fear was compounded for two reasons: we were in the dreaded basement, and they were trying to communicate with the dead. The fact that we lived across the road from a graveyard did nothing to improve my sense of security at these times. They would ask for a sign and we would wait. Finally something would happen—the fridge motor would click on behind us, or the neighbourhood boys would shine their flashlights through the basement windows, sending the teenage girls and the chubby little boy running and screaming up a flight of stairs to the security of the main floor of the house. Then of course the babysitters would announce that it was time for me to go to bed, completely oblivious to how these séances affected me.

It was no wonder that I had a lot of questions and fear regarding death and dying while growing up. Watching television shows like *The Ray Bradbury Trilogy* at that age was akin to receiving an alcoholic a drink: it might be hazardous to my well-being, but I could not resist. The episode I found most traumatic stayed with me for years. An older gentleman who lived with his nephew was ill, and the nephew was trying to kill him to inherit his millions. Eventually the nephew was successful, and his uncle was buried next door in the graveyard that was part of the estate. Just when the nephew thought everything was going as planned, he noticed an oil painting of the graveyard on the wall above the stairs. Instead of the original painting, this one showed a casket half out the ground. My fear mounted by the minute. The next time he looked, the painting showed the casket lid open. Next, a black figure was walking toward the house. That was all I could handle. I sat there with one eye on the television set and one on the graveyard across the street. As I write this I'm laughing, but at that time laughter was the farthest thing from my mind. The story ended with the discovery that the butler was switching the paintings so *he* could inherit the millions. It is now thirty years later, but I remember it as if it was yesterday. It came as no surprise that I took the long way home in an attempt to avoid the Dreaded Graveyard Walk By.

One other incident I wish to share from my childhood was one that involved the Ouija board. In my early teens I was often at a friend's house where we all loved to gather. I think everyone had such a place in their childhood, and Debbie's house was ours. Sometimes there were as many as nine or ten teenagers there at one time, yet we always felt welcomed. One day Debbie pulled out her mother's Ouija board, and we sat down to play. To me the very notion of what the board was designed for was ridiculous; it was impossible to make contact with the dead, however it might be fun to try. I don't remember what was spelled out, but I know that the planchette was moving around on its own. That was enough for me. If I couldn't explain the game, I certainly wouldn't play it anymore.

Debbie and I spent hours coming up with schemes designed to scare people. A good part of the day was spent rigging up her basement so that it seemed haunted. The rocking chair was set up to rock on its own. We had a Mrs. Beasley doll hanging by its neck so that when intended victims came downstairs, all they would see was the shadow bouncing off the walls. We knew we had pulled it off when Debbie's friend Christine came downstairs and within seconds ran up screaming. Now it was time to move on to the next setup.

After weeks of using the Ouija board, we became frightened mostly because of what Debbie's mother told us. Around this time, a couple of new kids moved into our small village, and their fear of the Ouija board was quite apparent. Our next con job involved two Ouija boards and the two new kids. We told them that we really didn't like the Ouija board and then proceeded to break it in front of them. Then we all went to the end of the street to burn and bury it. The second part of our plan was to get those two kids back to my house in order for them to see firsthand the second board displayed on my kitchen table, which we could see from outside the window. When we arrived, Debbie and I started screaming like there was no tomorrow. We kept saying, "It's evil! We can't kill it!" over and over. I know at the time the kids were scared stiff, but now as I write this it was really a lame attempt to scare two unsuspecting people.

Odds were they were probably scared more of the two lunatics screaming than the boards' powers.

On a Serious Note ...

Since discovering my ability of mediumship, I have used Ouija boards only a few times. I know from conversations with people over the years that there is a real fear surrounding Ouija boards. I think the Ouija board and other divination tools should be respected and not feared. No matter what we do in this life, I believe only our intent matters with regards to our actions. If you have a genuine curiosity about the board or spirit communication, try it but be respectful and educate yourself beforehand. If you are with people who are drinking alcohol and a Ouija board is pulled out, I suggest you get as far away from the environment as you can. When a person's thinking is impaired for any reason, it can quickly turn into a bad situation and often does. I would no more discuss spirit contact with someone in that condition than I would get in a car with them driving. I have too much respect for myself and those in the astral world. Regardless of what you have heard about the Ouija board or spirit communication, remember it is your intent that will determine the outcome.

Hearing Voices

Hearing voices and not seeing anyone can be a very unnerving experience. When it happened to me, it certainly was a puzzling and odd experience. In my mid twenties while home alone one afternoon, I walked through the kitchen of my home and could hear two distinct male voices having a conversation. Although I could not make out every word, I could tell that they spoke English. Where this was coming from, I wasn't sure. As I walked into my bedroom, the voices became louder and more distinct. After I checked to ensure the television set and radio were off, the conversation continued. Then I moved into the living room, to ascertain the stereo was off. The only other place in the house where we had any electronic equipment was downstairs, and although I had just come up, I returned to shut everything off, even unplugging the television set. When I headed back upstairs, I could still hear the chatter, so I looked outside. We live on a one-acre lot surrounded by farmland, and I could see no one around our property. After determining that the sound was originating from within the house, I continued to hunt for the source. Even though I unplugged the stereo and the radio, the conversation continued. I was drawn toward the headboard of our bed. It appeared to me that the voices seemed to come either from behind the bed or inside the wall. I was baffled, having never experienced this type of phenomenon before.

As a medium, when I hear voices, for the most part I hear them in my head, not as an exterior sound. The term for the ability to hear discarnate voices inside or outside the body is clairaudience, which means clear hearing. To this day I do not know what I heard or where it was coming from; all I know is that it was real.

Somehow these stories serve who I am; although I am unsure how, I just know they do. I simply thank God for the experiences that I had and continue to have. I view myself as an average person with many different faces, ever changing in my beliefs and behaviours. Slowly I am beginning to live more spiritually, strengthening my convictions to the point of appearing stubborn. It is hard to change my mind when it is set upon something. What I have come to learn is there are many different truths and realities out there. Every person has his or her own versions of reality, and none are wrong or right; they simply are. We feel the need to categorize them into a format that works for us. As an individual I am trying to grow to a point where I never attempt to change someone else's belief, however I admit that on occasion I still catch myself doing that and make myself stop. I know that this is all part of learning who I am; it is part of the process called creation. Instead of criticizing myself, I give thanks for the opportunity of seeing that it is not in my best interest to continue in this manner. To me success is being aware when you are doing or thinking something that is not creating the best possible you, then changing your thought or action to create a different outcome.

I know that when I am feeling good about myself nothing can go wrong, but as soon as I indulge in self-pity, anger or any emotion that is not of my highest thought, I attract negativity into my life. Even with this knowledge, I still wallow in self-pity or mild depression from time to time. One cannot know the good without experiencing the bad; one could not possibly know love if one did not know fear. Because of this law, we need to not condemn ourselves when we are not functioning at our highest or best. We need to simply realize this fact and work toward a more positive change. There is no need for blame in this world; we attract everything that happens to us. We must take responsibility for our lives and get on with them. If I am not happy with my life for any reason, I have no one to blame but myself. Regardless of what anyone else says or does to me, I have the free will to react or not to react. I can choose to take the higher road or get down and dirty. Too many years were lost to the down-and-dirty fights. I took great pride in plotting revenge. I now know that thinking in those terms only attracted more negativity to me and hurt me in the process.

My beliefs may not be yours. However, if anything I have relayed triggers you to take a more in-depth look at yourself, than I have achieved my goal. You may think this all sounds very much like a cliché and wonder how to change it from a belief to a practice. The answer is one step at a time. Spend time thinking about your beliefs, about how you react to stressful situations and fear. Tell yourself that you will catch yourself when you are not creating the highest and best you. Live from your heart and listen to your gut response to each situation in life.

Fears and phobias can isolate and cripple a person to the extent that it is impossible to function in society or, in milder cases, sustain a life of unhealthy patterns and choices. The only advice I can give to someone making choices that keep them in a pattern of non-growth is to review these choices by taking an honest look at these decisions and life patterns. Make a decision to not live out the charade any longer.

I have discovered that the only way to resolve fears and phobias is to look head-on at what you fear most. By keeping something in the dark or continuously pushing it away, you only give it life. Nothing is ever frightening or harmful when light is shed on it. I can't tell you how many times I put something off or blew a situation all out of proportion, only to discover, when I could no longer deny the situation and was forced to address it, that ultimately it was not so bad. That is when I would ask myself, "Why didn't I just deal with it when it first happened?"

By fearing something and trying to push it away, I ultimately made it far more real and a much worse situation than it needed to be. At one time in my life, the thought of public speaking would paralyze me with fear. Knowing I would be speaking in front of a large crowd could make me sick to my stomach. Once I faced this fear head-on; rationalized the worst case scenarios and confronted my fear by leaping off the edge of my comfort zone and into an unchartered territory, I realized I did not fall and actually soared to greater heights. I can honestly tell you that I love public speaking now and relish the idea of doing more of it in the years to come. Quite simply I have come to the conclusion that I do not want fear running my life, and I do not want to get to the end of my life and say I wish I had.

I have since realized that regardless of what point I am at in my life, I am indeed progressing forward. We humans tend to be very judgmental with ourselves and with others. I know each of us has looked at another's life and said, "What a waste," but the truth is that people progress at their own rate and direction. What may take one person ten life lessons to finally learn may take someone else only one. The difference is one's level of awareness. Because life cannot cease to exist, neither can progress; no matter how small the movement forward, there will always be a forward motion in everyone's life. When we make a judgment about ourselves or someone else, that is all it is—our judgment. It doesn't make our opinion right; on the contrary, we are often wrong.

I recently had a client in my office for a reading. Todd had lost his girlfriend, Leah, to ovarian cancer. After his consultation, Todd told me he struggled with how active, how young, how full of life and how healthy Leah was, only to die at the age of thirty-four from cancer. He told me he couldn't help but feel anger when he saw a street person, or perhaps a drug addict or drunk, and they were still alive but his precious Leah was not. I told him that his feelings were very natural but very judgmental. I explained to him that although it did not seem fair, he had no idea of that street person's life purpose. Neither did he know the history and the story that put that person on the street or to drugs. I believed he was able to see his situation in a new light, even if for just a minute.

When I look back on my childhood and see my life for what it is, I would not change a thing. I choose to view my past as a beautiful mosaic work of art. When I examine the mosaic piece by piece, I can see the rough textures and sharp contrast that appear at times as far from beautiful as one can imagine. Upon stepping back and looking at my life as a whole, I see a beautiful piece of art, one I would not change.

Chapter 4
VISITATIONS

During many of my discernments, those in the spirit world talk about coming to visit their loved ones in dreams. Normally one might dismiss these dreams as vivid imaginings or wishful thinking on the part of the bereaved family member, but they are very real. When we sleep we have let our guard down in a sense, and a relaxed state enables us to perceive things that cannot normally be seen or felt. Our brain wave patterns vary depending on the state of sleep. It is during these times that our loved ones find it easiest to make a connection. In order for you to be able to define your own visitation experience, there are a few significant points to look for.

1) The vividness of the encounter is so clear, so strong that you will never forget the impact of or the circumstances surrounding the visit. Even years later, the memory will remain clear, crisp and very colourful. Recalling the smallest details will take no effort at all.

2) During a visitation the colours you experience often seem more real, vivid and brighter than anything you have experienced in the physical sense.

3) The message you are given brings peace and contentment, and it may even answer questions you have. The message may simply be the overall impact of the visitation.

Another Good-bye

My first visitation occurred nearly twenty-four years ago, in November 1986. My paternal grandfather had been in a nursing home for a couple of years and suffered from Alzheimer's disease. The last time that I visited him was in June of that year, and I was shocked that he looked much older than his seventy years; due to years of arthritic degeneration, his gnarled hands could barely move. Alzheimer's had also taken its toll, because he did not know who I was. However he recognized my sister, Tracey, and her name was one of the few words he could say. Because walking was only possible on a good day, he remained bedridden. The staff informed us that Grandpa was getting worse and would not last much longer. Upon hearing this, it caused me to reflect on how selfish I had been in not making an effort to see him over the past few months, and now I never would get the opportunity to say good-bye.

That night after I had gone to bed, my grandfather came to visit me. The visit was so dear to my heart that I can recount the events as if it was last night. I was standing at the foot of a bed looking down at a man I knew to be my grandfather. He lay there looking old and frail but was able to call my name. I went to the side of his bed and told him I was sorry I had not been to see him in months. I was crying as I held his hand, but with so much love in his eyes, he told me everything was okay. I told him I loved him and that even though I was sorry, I was also happy to have the chance to say good-bye.

I awoke in tears, sure that my grandfather had passed away. I called Grandmother and asked if Grandpa had passed away. She said she had not heard anything from the nursing home and could only assume that everything was the same. I told her of my visitation and how real it was, and she thought it was nice that I had such a wonderful dream. To her that was all it was, but I knew it was far more than just a dream. My grandfather passed away the following day.

Though his wake and funeral were sad occasions, I was grateful to this fine man for finding a way to remove the guilt I had felt for not seeing him one last time. My grandfather came to me in a way I cannot fully understand, but it allowed us to say our good-byes. There is no stronger bond than love, and there is no distance or dimension where love does not exist. My grandfather gave me the greatest gift possible, and he did this when he was at his weakest and in an unconscious state. He transcended the physical barriers to visit me in my dream.

My Pennies from Heaven

When we arrived at my grandparents' home the evening Grandpa passed away, I had mixed feelings over his death. I always loved my grandfather, but I never seemed to be close to him. Though I did enjoy seeing him, my visits were primarily for my grandmother because she was the one with whom I had the real connection. During his funeral as I listened to the minister talk about him, I realized I never knew him. The eulogy told of his being a founding member and one of the builders of the very church we were sitting in. He had been a groundskeeper at the local cemetery, a past president of the Royal Canadian Legion—the list of accomplishments went on. I was now seeing a new side of him. This was a very impressive person that I had missed out on knowing.

The day following my grandfather's death, Grandma handed out little keepsakes of his to each of his grandchildren. She gave me two white handkerchiefs, a framed certificate and a wallet that had seen better days. On opening the wallet, I found two pennies. The first had been minted in 1916, the second in 1986. What makes this astounding is that my grandfather was born in 1916 and died in 1986. I knew Grandpa was giving me another sign that all was well. I decided I was not to keep the coins; instead I would use them to show my grandfather I had received his message. On Sunday night I went to the church where Grandpa's body was on display. An empty church was intimidating enough, but knowing that Grandpa's body was awaiting me in the darkness was unnerving. I walked forward slowly, and with every step I fought the desire to turn and run. When I finally reached the front, the man lying in the open coffin looked twenty years younger. I stood there trembling as I talked to him—I was now having a conversation with a dead body, but this didn't seem odd to me. As I told him how I was feeling, a wonderful sense of peace washed over me. I remember thinking I had never touched a dead body before, so before I could change my mind I reached into the coffin and wrapped the two coins into his cold stiff hands and said my last good-byes. The cold, lifelessness of his body is something I will not forget, yet this simple act brought me closure. I thanked him for my pennies from Heaven.

I Am Just Fine!

Most visitations occur from deceased loved ones. My grandmother came visiting about one week after her death while my grieving of the loss of this special lady was quite acute. At the time of her passing, I was not yet aware of the spirit world. Even though I had not experienced it firsthand, in my heart I believed that life continued on after death and that my grandmother was okay.

In this particular visitation, I got out of bed and walked across the hall to the kitchen door, where I could see my Grandmother and her sister Mable, who was still very much alive, walking in the front entrance of our home. I stood there in disbelief. I could not believe Grandma was approaching me with her arms outstretched. We hugged and kissed as we had so many times before, and then I said, "Grandma you're dead—what are you doing here?"

She looked me square in the eye while still holding my shoulders and said, "Chris, I am just fine," and she laughed and gave me a warm, reassuring smile. I hugged her again and told her I missed her then, and Grandma turned and walked back down the stairs to the front door. I immediately woke up. In the short time we visited, she confirmed she was fine and happy.

What made this even more powerful was hearing the following weekend from Aunt Molly that she had also dreamed of her mother that week. When

I asked what her dream was about, she said her mother sat straight up in the casket and looked directly at her. My aunt was startled and cried out, "Mom you are dead. How can you be sitting up?" Grandma's response was, "I am just fine." When we had compared our dreams, we were amazed that Grandma used the same wording with each of us to convey the fact that all was indeed well.

There are also visitations that can occur while one is wide awake; these forms of communication come in many ways. Perhaps you have ever been watching television alone or have been engaged in a quiet activity, and out of the corner of your eye you see someone pass through the room; when you look, there is no one there, so you dismiss it as your imagination. This phenomenon happens because you are relaxed, in a state similar to being in a mild form of sleep or trance. Your brain waves are at a different level in this state, and you are able to perceive things when you are not concentrating on them.

Communications happen through electricity as well. In our house, hall lights go on and off at different times, our television set switches channels for no apparent reason and on occasion items in the kitchen fly off a shelf to land five or six feet away. Scents can also play a large part in a conscious visitation. The smell of a familiar perfume, a pipe or maybe the fumes of alcohol can all be signs that you are not alone. In my house we have had situations where a strong odour seems to originate from the middle of a room. On one particular occasion, it was the stench of something burning in the centre of the kitchen in a two by eight foot area. We could walk through it and, once outside the two-foot-wide space, could not smell it. Within half an hour it was gone completely, and we attributed it to my wife's grandma, who was famous for burning food in the kitchen. She was known to start cooking dinner and then walk away, forgetting the stove was on.

Another form of communication that I have experienced occurs as I am about to drift off to sleep. Out of nowhere a voice will yell out my name. I have to sit up and look around the room because it takes me a few seconds to get my bearings. The voice is so loud and clear that I actually think someone is calling me from the foot of my bed. When these strange occurrences happen, my wife and I often take time to reflect on what is going on around us. I use these messages as tools by making myself more aware of my surroundings and paying particular attention to my children's whereabouts. These forms of communication are to be appreciated, welcomed and cherished. Our loved ones do not stop loving us because they have physically died. We are bound together by a strong bond that even death can not sever. Nothing can prevent those who love us from trying to communicate and help whenever possible or permitted.

If an unpleasant event happens, we may wonder why someone from the spirit world did not help. The truth is they often do try to assist, but we are so wrapped up in our lives that we do not pay attention to the signs. These signs can be as subtle as a breeze or as drastic as knocking the wind out of us. There are also times when those in the spirit world can not intervene because what is about to take place is designed as a period of personal and spiritual growth for us, even if we cannot see it at the time. It isn't until we reflect on what has taken place that we are able to see the positive aspects of the lesson. Some people never see or experience this positive side because that requires them to be very honest with themselves. You can lie to others and you can live in denial, but you can never lie to yourself and not be aware of it. Your soul knows what's right and wrong for you, and no amount of denial can change this.

Visitations can occur at any moment in time. Regardless whether the intended recipient is awake or asleep; visitations can be life-changing gifts that provide indescribable comfort and peace of mind to people coping with unimaginable loss. They are real interactions with the spirit world that need to be cherished and appreciated for what they are: bonds of eternal love.

Chapter 5
GOING PUBLIC

The time had come for me to go public with my gift. In July 1997 my friend Debbie was having a week of open houses, seminars and drop-in nights at her new age bookstore called Far From Normal. She had asked me several weeks earlier if I would give a talk one night that week on mediumship. I was unprepared for this request but was flattered to have been asked, even though Debbie didn't know any other mediums. My first response was that I was not yet ready to take this next step, but Debbie convinced me that I was ready by reminding me that the opportunity was presenting itself for a reason.

I was booked into the Friday night slot, and it felt right. I spent the next few weeks preparing for my first public appearance. I listed the topics I planned to cover and went over it in my mind several times a day. Because I didn't want it to sound rehearsed, I put my notes in point form. It had been less than a year since I had discovered this gift, and I was now taking a major step forward. I remained calm that day until about thirty minutes before I was to start. My nerves started to get the better of me, and once again doubt reared its ugly head. People started arriving, so I went into Debbie's office to meditate and prepare. Fortunately this seemed to work; in no time I was walking out into a room full of people. The room's capacity was approximately twenty-five people, and that evening there were twenty-seven. That may not seem like a very large crowd, but to me that evening, it felt like thousands. I took my place at the front of the room and introduced myself. The evening flew by, and I felt that it had gone well. This was confirmed when the group expressed how much they had enjoyed my talk and how surprised they were to hear this was my first speaking engagement.

At the conclusion of the night, some of the people came up to me to ask more personal questions. One woman named Donna seemed very troubled. I told her there was a woman standing behind her who was telling me her name was Mary. She said, "That's right," and began to cry. Mary was her mother, who had recently passed, and Donna explained that since her passing, the family ties were falling apart fast. I told Donna that her mother was fine and that she would also be fine. I continued to relay Mary's message about the day her father rushed her mother to the hospital. In the haste and confusion, he had accidentally knocked a figurine off a table and broke it. Mary explained that Donna had this ornament fixed. Donna began crying uncontrollably at this bit of information and asked, "How could you possibly know this?"

I explained once again that her mother was now standing beside her and that she really was fine. Mary told her daughter not to focus on her parents' personal items and not to put too much importance on things. She went on to explain that when Donna's father knocked the ornament off the table, he had been totally consumed with helping his loving wife. This figurine was all she really needed because it was a symbol of her parents' love. Material items may be important to other family members, but Donna had what really counted.

Mary knew how to handle the situation, and she did it with such love that Donna felt great relief. She thanked me, and after talking for about thirty minutes, she left. Donna has been back to see me twice since that night. I know that Donna had a hard time coming to terms with death and the loss of her parents, but the messages from her family helped address her concerns and put her in a better place.

Five weeks later I had my first booking. The client was unknown to me at that time, and the following account is taken from notes written after the session.

September 3, 1997

My client's name was Sherry (for reasons of privacy, I will not use her real name). Her appointment was made through my friend Debbie's store, and when she arrived, I knew that I had seen her before. I knew little else about her—not her family name, where she lived or what she expected from me. The only thing I did know was that she worked in town. I offered her a cup of tea, wanting to make sure at least one of us was comfortable and relaxed. After a few minutes of conversation and meditation, I was ready to begin.

The first person to come through was a lady who identified herself as Beth. Sherry told me that was her great-grandmother Elizabeth. She was from England, I said.

Sherry confirmed this. Sherry's great-grandmother talked about a child being born to one person and raised by another. Sherry explained that this was her father.

Next came Sherry's grandmother. Sherry said her name was Alice. I received an image of a very neat, proper and well-dressed lady wearing pearls. Then an image of June Cleaver came forth. I told Sherry that the woman I was seeing was middle-aged, even though she died much older, and she was a quiet lady with not a lot to say.

A young girl came in next, and her age would switch from a little girl to a teenager. She talked about grade three and how one particular boy was constantly mean to her. She told me her name was Candace, or Candy, she said with a laugh.

Sherry said that she had one classmate known as Candace who, as far as she knew, had grown into an adult and then lost touch. This part of the reading meant nothing to her.

The next presence to come through was Sherry's other grandmother. I described her as a large woman black tie-up shoes, and the sole of her left shoe was thicker than the right one. She was sitting on the front porch of her house with a cane resting between her legs. She waved a Bible at me, so I asked Sherry if she was a religious lady. Sherry said that her grandmother was extremely religious. I described her hairstyle and the fact that I was picking up some kind of French background. Sherry again verified all of this.

Sherry then asked if her grandfather was available or around. I described a smaller man who was balding with hair around the lower back of his head, very neat and tidy. His shirt was tucked in and he wore slippers. He was smoking a pipe and rolling cigarettes. Sherry verified all of this except the cigarettes. He told me that he was not nearly as strong in his religious beliefs. Again Sherry said this was correct.

I told Sherry she had two guides present; one was a female schoolmaster and one was an angel of light, and both represented her personality and lifestyle. Just before concluding, Sherry asked if there were any messages for anyone in her family. I sat and waited and then received the name Wes. I asked Sherry if there was someone with a "W" name in her family. She wasn't sure, but when I told her the name I was getting was Wes, she said, "Yes, of course, I know Wes." I delivered the message from Wes and knew I had done my part.

That concluded the session.

After Sherry left with her cassette recording in hand, I sat down to take in what had just transpired. I felt a level of accomplishment I had never experienced before, and I knew I was now starting on my new life's path, which would lead me to the life I was always meant to live. For the first time in my life, I remember truly feeling a remarkable sense of satisfaction, knowing I had just helped a fellow human being in such a unique and uplifting way. I wanted to experience that feeling more.

When I look back on my introduction to working as a medium publicly, I realize I possessed one key element that made my experience so rewarding and successful. That element I possessed was faith. Faith gave me the courage to speak my truth to a room full of strangers, and it gave me the confidence to sit one-on-one and provide life-changing messages for Sherry. I have learned since those early days that success in all aspects of life requires faith. Faith in one's self, faith in life and faith that no matter what unfolds in life, it will be okay.

With my first public speaking engagement and private session under my belt, I now looked to the future with optimism and had my focus set on going public with my ability of mediumship. There would be no looking back.

Chapter 6
DELIVERING ON A PROMISE

August 27, 1997

I woke up at 4:00 a.m. with excitement building and anticipation brimming over. This was the day I was going to the State of New York to visit a small community known as Lily Dale. Lily Dale is a picturesque town nestled in western New York State. It is not a typical town by any stretch of the imagination; instead this town is a spiritual community comprised of mediums, healers and mediums in training.

I couldn't wait to get there, so by 6:00 a.m. our group consisting of five friends and Kim and I were off. We drove through the Lily Dale gates at 9:30 that morning. I didn't know what I was expecting, but this surely wasn't it. I knew the quickest way to disappointment in life was to have expectations about something, but it was exactly what I had done. Lily Dale was comprised of a total of about seven small, dirt roads with quaint cottages all in a row. There was a gift store or two and a few larger, two-story homes on the edge of the community. We located a directory and schedule of daily events, and then all seven of us headed straight to the healing temple at the north side of the spiritualist resort. We picked up some literature and sat down in different rows, waiting for the healing session to begin. While sitting I noticed the atmosphere in the small, white church was very peaceful. A wonderful energy filled this room and the people in it. When the service started, several healers came up to the front of the temple and gave a brief introduction to the types of healing being offered. Many people went up to receive healing, and when it was my turn, I sat down with my back to the practitioner. The combination of angelic music in the background, gifted practitioners volunteering their services and the wonderful presence of spirit all came together to create one of the most sensational healing experiences I have ever had.

The practitioner began running her hands about two inches above my body. She whispered very quietly that I had a blockage in my throat chakra, and she started to remove it. Within seconds I felt my throat begin to close up, and I was unable to breathe comfortably. Then I felt a strange pop in my thorax, followed by something leaving through the back of my neck. It was incredible. I felt lighter and happier.

After all of us had experienced some form of healing, we left the temple and walked to the far end of the resort to a place in the woods called the stump. Walking along a groomed trail that included a pet cemetery, I noticed the energy building up the closer we got to our destination. The stump was situated in the centre of an outdoor theatre surrounded by row upon row of wooden benches.

I don't fully recall what significance this place held, but to the local residents it appeared to have importance. As I sat waiting for the mediums to begin, my attention was drawn to a man in spirit standing behind my right shoulder. The demonstration was starting when this gentleman tapped me on the shoulder to get my attention. He proceeded to divulge things about his life that he wanted me to relay to someone in particular. I tried to concentrate on what was happening up front, but this man was very persistent. He constantly poked me, telling me things and trying to exact a promise that I would relay his messages. I had no intention of walking up to a stranger and telling him or her anything, but he was one of the most unrelenting spirits I have ever met. Finally, in desperation I promised to do as he asked. He kept pointing to an older woman sitting across the aisle from me. It was only after my promise that he stood back and left me alone.

At the completion of the demonstration, I stood up to leave when my new friend came back and reminded me of my promise. I returned to the lady he'd pointed out and said, "Excuse me." She turned to face me, and even though I was a very nervous, I began my message. "I have never done anything like this, but I feel you were hoping for a message here today, and you didn't get one." She said this was true but that it was okay. I told her I believed I had a message for her and asked if she would like me to relay it. When she replied that she would, I began by telling her of how, throughout the service, this man refused to leave me alone until I agreed to talk to her.

I described the gentleman who was now standing beside her as balding with the first initial of his name as "J." As I finished relaying this information, one of the woman's companions began to cry. She said, "Oh my God, it really is him—it's Joe." I asked the older lady if this was her husband, because he was telling me there is a very close bond with her. She informed me that no, this man was her brother. I went on to tell her that he kept showing me a scene in which he entered a blue car. I didn't understand the significance of this, but because he was playing it over and over, it seemed important that I pass it on to her. She told me her brother loved to drive his car, and yes, it was blue. I continued by telling her that he said he was fine and that he was around her a lot at night. He showed me an image of this lady sitting in a chair and reading beside a small table and lamp; behind her was the entrance to her kitchen, and music was playing. I let her know that he enjoyed these quiet moments and assured her once again that he was well.

With the message complete, I went on to say I hoped I had not upset them, because this was not my intent. The sister of the man in spirit said they were not at all upset and thanked me for what I had done. With that I turned and walked away. I don't think I will ever forget the wonderful feeling I had—a feeling of accomplishment and knowing I had really helped someone with my ability. What stands out in my mind was the incredible self-confidence I had discovered in myself that enabled me to deliver this man's messages to his sister.

Not all of Lily Dale was a great experience for me. I am a person who is naturally skeptical, and I had a hard time accepting all of the mediums I saw there that day as being legitimate. A negative feeling came over me once we left the stump, and during the next two demonstrations my negativity increased without my understanding why. As time passed, I grew less comfortable with my surroundings and became very anxious to leave. Whether I was right or wrong about my feelings that day, I had to honour them. If I didn't listen to myself and follow my intuition, how could I expect anyone to trust what I had to say?

I left Lily Dale with mixed emotions, but I cannot deny the overwhelming experiences I had there. Everything happens for a reason, and the healing I had received earlier that day removed a block in my throat chakra, possibly helped me to deliver a message to a stranger from her brother. Since that visit I've heard many good things about Lily Dale and would suggest to anyone who feels compelled to visit, to leave his or her expectations at home and enjoy it for what it is: a quaint, spiritual resort.

Please Tell Heather I Am Okay ...

Being asked to do a favour for someone is usually very simple. Having to pass a message on to someone whose loved one has just passed over is much more difficult. There have been times during my career as a medium that spirits have come through, asking my clients to relay messages to a loved one. When this first happened, I did not give much thought to the impact such a request might have on the person being asked. I always stressed the importance of such a request, but until it happened to me, I never completely understood how large an undertaking this was.

On March 16, 2000, in the middle of a reading with two female clients, a man from spirit walked in and said, "It's Pat, it's Pat." I told my two clients about the gentleman standing between them who said his name was Pat. They both shook their heads no. "He tells me that he's lived in New Lowell and that he passed from cancer." Because my clients themselves were from

New Lowell, I felt at least one of them must know him. They still insisted they did not. Finally the man from spirit said, "I'm not here for them—I am here for you. You know me. I'm Pat. You know, Pat and Heather."

"It seems that our friend here is coming through with a message for me during your session," I explained. Pat laughed; he was very pleased with the fact that not only had he grabbed my attention, but he had done so on someone else's time. I finally realized Pat and his wife, Heather, were a couple I had met on a few occasions when in business for myself. I also realized I had typed his death notice for the newspaper one week earlier without realizing I knew him.

"I need you to contact Heather for me and let her know I am doing okay," he continued.

I froze at his request. I explained to my clients what was taking place and what was being asked of me, and one of the ladies said, "I'm glad I'm not you—how are you possibly going to do it?" I had no idea. Pat asked me to go to his memorial service the following day and talk to Heather.

I barely knew this lady, and I was not about to walk into the service and say, "Excuse me, I heard from your husband last night—and oh, by the way, he still has a wonderful sense of humour." I was also concerned that his death had been so recent that Heather would be in a fragile state of mind. I knew the importance of his request and realized I had an obligation not only to Pat and Heather but to myself as well. How could I expect others to relay messages in the future if I myself could not find the strength and love to do so?

While driving home that night, I asked for direction from Grey Owl. I told him I had no intention of showing up at the memorial service the next day. In his wonderful and compassionate way, Grey Owl suggested I write a letter and take it to the funeral home early the next morning. I thought this idea was a good one because I would be able to put on paper what I wouldn't be able to say face to face. I wasn't worried what Pat's wife might think of me, but I was concerned with how this would affect her. Because it had been such a short time, she likely hadn't had time to deal with Pat's passing, but Pat assured me she was ready and it would not hurt her in any way. Early the next morning, I went into work and typed the letter, which I delivered to the funeral home a short time later.

After typing the letter, I shared the situation with my co-worker and watched as a look of fear crossed her face, but after a few minutes she said, "I don't think the spirits would have you do something that would hurt anyone. This must be really tough on you."

I drove my letter to the funeral home and asked the funeral director if he'd give it to Heather Jordan at the conclusion of the service, and I left. A feeling of relief washed over me as I drove out of the parking lot, but when two weeks passed and I had not heard from Heather, I began to wonder what impact it had had on her. Had she even believed me?

The following morning while at my desk, I heard someone come into the office. I looked up to see Heather standing there, and my heart jumped into my throat. I stood up walked toward her, saying, "I am so sorry to hear about Pat." As tears began to fill her eyes, I managed to say, "How are you doing?"

"I am doing fine," she replied, beginning to smile.

"I guess you want to know about the letter I sent you." I said.

"Yeah," she said quietly.

I proceeded to recount the events from two weeks earlier, including my doubts and fears about doing what was asked of me. Heather told me her first reaction was one of sadness and upset. She started to read the letter and then threw it across the table. Her mother picked it up and read it, saying, "This is garbage;

who would do this to you?" Heather explained how she had picked up the letter numerous times over the next couple of days and read it again and again. Could this be true, or was it really a cruel hoax? Something finally told her that it was at least worth looking into. We talked for about twenty minutes that day, and I told her to call me if she ever needed anything.

About two weeks later, I met with Heather and her mother at a local doughnut shop to talk with them at their request. Heather's mother had no idea of what to expect, so I explained what I could about my gift, and then people from spirit started making their presence known to me. I relayed several messages for Heather's mother, and she was able to confirm everyone and everything that came through that day. She was astonished with some of the things that were said, things her daughter was not even aware of.

Then Pat came through. He stood next to Heather with a confident grin of what he had accomplished from the other side. I told Heather he was standing there with one hand in his pocket jingling his keys or coins. He was laughing and wanted her to know he would never leave her. He also let her know he would never again come through me to communicate with her; he said she could do it herself. When it was time for me to leave, Heather's mother was still shaking her head in disbelief.

Heather has since told me that her mother, who was very skeptical of my letter, of me in general and of my abilities, is no longer a skeptic. This was a very difficult experience for me to go through, yet it was so rewarding and fulfilling connecting two people who loved each other very deeply. Thank you, Pat!

I have shared two very unique and difficult requests asked of me in this chapter, both of which detail the responsibility and difficult choices I as a medium had to face and ultimately conquer. I learned early on that my feelings and my comfort level are secondary to those in spirit. My job is to be the voice for those that have been silenced through physical death. To do that well, I must not let my personal feelings of discomfort and my ego overshadow the bigger need of those in spirit.

Chapter 7
HOW SPIRITS COMMUNICATE

When I first started working with my ability of mediumship, the spirits made their presence known by passing through me. When they came into the room or were ready to be noticed, they would physically travel through my body. This physical contact with the spirit world always left me with an amazing feeling. The strength of the spirit could be measured by the amount of energy that passed through me. When the message was serious or of vital importance, the spirit would arrive with undeniable force, and there was no mistaking the direction that the discernment was going to take. Because I was so new to this form of communication and was such a skeptic, if I received just the messages without the physical impact, it would have been a lot less effective and may have taken me twice as long as necessary to repeat what I was being told.

As time passed and I grew more accustomed to knowing and trusting the process, the physical contact became less and less. This actually saddened me because it was such a wonderful feeling. During many of my discernments, even after I had identified the visitor and successfully communicated many messages, I would begin to doubt myself and would ask for confirmation by way of a pass-through. The answer would be a resounding no, and in a loving way the spirit world would explain that I had passed that level of communication and would not return to it. There were bigger and better things ahead of me; I must have faith in them and learn to have more trust in my abilities.

As a young, budding medium, I did not have the opportunity of working with a study group or a mentor, but I did have the fortitude to continue my journey. Even with all the doubts, faith moved me forward. One good thing about working independently is that I did not pick up bad habits from anyone else, and neither did I adopt any beliefs that were not my own. My centre of truth rested solely on my own shoulders. Although books were my best study guide, advising me what to expect, how to meditate and how to believe in myself, the actual spirit world was my classroom. I learned many forms of spirit communication, the most common methods being clairvoyance, clairaudience and clairsentience.

Clairvoyance is the method of "clear seeing" with your mind's eye. This takes place in the form of pictures I view, whether my eyes are open or closed, and the images could be projected in front of me like a movie playing on a screen, or it may be pictures or symbols flashed in front of me. The closest example I can give for clairvoyance is daydreaming. Think of the times your mind has wandered off, and you are in your favourite vacation spot, or maybe you are reliving a happy occasion from the past. It plays out in front of you or in your mind as a movie, full of colour and very real. When spirit uses this form of communication with me, I see images, pictures and sometimes whole scenes play out in my mind's eye. I then relay to the client what I am being shown.

Clairaudience is "clear hearing." This method of communication is the ability to hear conversations, words and sounds from the spirit world. Sometimes the sounds are external, which means I hear them outside my body, but for the most part I tend to receive this form of communication in my mind. The best way to describe this is for you to have a conversation with yourself. Ask yourself a question out loud and wait for the answer in your head; it should be loud and clear. I am sure you have been on the verge of drifting off to sleep and then hear your name called out, and you sit straight up in your bed only to realize no one is in the room with you. This I believe is clairaudience at work. Quite simply, people are more receptive to this form of communication while in a meditative state. A person who is in the process of drifting off to sleep is replicating a meditative state, and spirits can access your awareness more easily at these times. For me clairaudience is anything but clear. This form of spirit communication can be very subtle in nature and can take years for a medium to become accustomed to the meanings and intricacies of this form of communication.

Clairsentience means "clear knowing or clear feeling." Have you ever just known something where there was seemingly no way you could have known it, such as when someone is lying to you and you have no proof, yet with every fiber of your being you know this person is not being truthful? Perhaps you have felt like someone has been staring at you or felt like someone is with you, standing right next to you, even though when you turn to look, no one is there. Have you ever had a strong sensation and thought about a certain person, and within the hour that person calls you? These examples are all forms of clairsentience. For me, when working with a client, spirit uses clairsentience in almost every session. Each reading starts long before my client has even entered my office or picked up the phone to call me. Spirits tend to first grab my attention by indicating through clairsentience that they are in the room with me. I will get a physical pull by the spirits indicating they have somewhat plugged in to my energy field and awareness, thus creating a mental meeting of sorts. I get impressions, feelings and a pull of energy directing me to where the spirit is located physically in the room. The mental awareness of gender and generation often comes flooding into my body and mind immediately after the original contact has taken place. These instances are followed quite often by the cause of physical death, which when all combined together, provides me with the ground work of information to start the client's session. This form of communication from spirit is critical in the way I work, and regardless whether I am working one on one with a client in my office or in a theatre filled with hundreds of people, the process remains the same. What I learned early on is that a client's mother or father's vibration in spirit has a different pull and frequency level than a spouses or sibling's energy would be. The same principles apply to a young energy, such as a child or grandchild communicating from spirit. After almost fifteen years of doing this work, I have become quite proficient at sorting out and interpreting the energies from spirit.

When I am communicating with the spirit world, these are the three forms of contact I primarily use. I have no say in or control over which format will be used. The spirit world just knows best which will be the most effective. Many times a session will be comprised of all three forms, and sometimes an entire reading will consist of only one. The one thing that is consistent with every session is that the spirit world uses something familiar to trigger me to get their messages across. They use mental images and smells, and they access my memory bank and pull out circumstances that are similar to the messages they are bringing to the person sitting in front of me. They will often pull out a memory of my grandparents, their home or even a scene from a movie that I have watched in the past that directly relates to the message I need to deliver at that time.

Spirits are masterful communicators and know what needs to be delivered and how to get their messages across to their loved ones. If you ever decide to sit with a medium, please understand that your loved ones in spirit have their own agenda, and no matter what you believe you are looking to get out of the reading, those in spirit follow their agenda and not yours. Experience has shown me that spirits use a series of validations throughout a session to create a shift in my client's awareness and belief system. Some validations are jaw-dropping and life changing; other messages are very subtle and, only when combined with the total experience of the client's reading, create the comfort and realization that life is eternal.

Spirit Rescue—Rising to the Occasion

When I was starting out with my mediumship, I had a network of good friends who had interests in the paranormal, spirituality and the big question, "What's the meaning of life?" We started meeting weekly to enjoy a night of conversation, meditation and exercises. I discovered my friends were quite willing to take part in sessions of spirit contacts. This fact delighted me because it gave me much-needed practice while re-acquainting them with loved ones and spirit guides.

My friend, Debbie, was in the process of opening her book store in a new location. We decided to hold a séance in the store. There were five of us that first evening, and it started out with relatives from spirit coming through with messages for those in attendance. After about an hour or so, a new energy made its presence known to me. I could not determine who or what it was, but I did detect that it was a male. As I began to inquire about our new visitor, a feeling of terror (energy) shot from the top of my head, down the back of my neck and down my spine. Within seconds I apologized to those in attendance and said I could not continue. It was 8:40 p.m., and I told my friends I had never felt fear such as I had just experienced. I could not continue and could not explain the sensation properly. We quickly cleaned up the basement and moved upstairs, where we discussed what had just happened to me, and I tried once again to explain it. I had felt a cold, swirling motion behind my back that seemed to shoot down my backside. As we stood upstairs preparing to leave, Lynda said that she could feel a swirl of energy coming from the centre of the room. We all congregated in that area and felt an incredibly strong and negative energy swirl around us. We remained another half an hour, and still the energy persisted. We finally said our good-byes and I thought that was the end of it.

When I arrived home, I raced inside to tell Kim what had happened in the hope she would be able to shed some light on what I had felt. Kim is many things to me, but she is always the voice of reason. I found her in the bedroom reading and said, "You will never guess what happened tonight." She looked startled, but I was too involved in my story to pay much attention. I continued, explaining the best I could, until she stopped me saying she too had experienced something very unnerving that night. It had just passed 8:30, and after putting the boys to bed, she went to our basement to change the channel on the satellite. After leaving the television room, she walked about two feet into the basement hallway and then stopped, frozen in her tracks. She told me it felt as if someone was standing directly behind her; she was startled that when she turned to look, no one was there. She felt very unnerved by this and ran upstairs to check on our children, and then she retreated to our bedroom. She said she had never felt frightened before in our house; this was a first.

I do not believe it was merely coincidence that at approximately the same time we both experienced the same feeling in two different places. I know now that the spirit world has an incredible way of working, and this was its way of getting my attention. Not only had I experienced it, but my wife had as well. As we talked about the impact of feeling such a negative spirit, the more we vented, the more I realized what we felt was neither negative nor bad—it was troubled. What I had on my hands was a male spirit who was in trouble! I do not believe in evil spirits, but I had a need to categorize him as we do to everyday people around us. I had misjudged the situation.

The next morning I took a book to work with me about spirit communication. As I read a chapter on helping spirits who are trapped, it became quite clear what I needed to attempt. I called the people who were present the previous night to discuss what had happened and also to talk about meeting as soon as possible to try to help this troubled soul. Everyone agreed to do whatever they could to help. The next morning at 8 a.m., we met at the store and once again went downstairs. We started with a prayer of protection, and within minutes the spirit in question made his presence known to us. He was so powerful that this time even Lynda felt his energy. I remained calm and took charge. I apologized for my previous behaviour and explained that we were here to help him. He began by telling me his name and that this had been his home for the last eight decades. I told him that he had two daughters that were waiting in spirit for him. I informed him that all he had to do was look for the white light, and once he found it, he should go toward it. I promised a family reunion was awaiting him once he got there and calmly reassured him that he had no reason to stay here; only goodness lay ahead.

Suddenly in the far corner of the room, a bright, white light appeared from the ceiling, and three people emerged. Two women and a man stood there with open arms, watching as I directed this poor soul toward the light that bathed the room. I told him that I would walk him through it all and that he would not be alone even for a second. I directed him to look for the three people waiting for him and then felt his energy swirl upward toward the ceiling. Just as I spoke to let my friends know he was gone, he appeared in the corner of the room. With a smile he looked back and thanked me, and then he turned with his family and walked into the light. As quickly as it had started, it was over. My first experience of helping a spirit stranded here in the physical realm went relatively smoothly. I know from the few discussions I had with this particular man that he died traumatically and was confused. He did not elaborate on how he had died, but I felt he could not adjust to his new surroundings.

I am telling you this story for two reasons: to explain that spirits can be confused about their deaths, especially if their passing is tragic, but more important to show how quickly we humans jump to conclusions. This man did what he thought was necessary to get my attention, and he succeeded by getting my wife's attention as well. This fact, more than any other, made me realize I was dealing with something unknown. I misinterpreted this man's original intention and that taught me a lesson I will never forget. When people ask me if I believe in evil spirits, I tell them I do not. Many people find this hard to believe because they feel they have experienced evil entities firsthand. I ask them to suppose that what they experienced wasn't an evil spirit but a troubled spirit, and then I recount my tale. I am thankful I had this experience and what I learned from it. The outcome benefitted not only the trapped spirit but me as well, and perhaps those who believe in evil spirits too.

The trapped soul discussed in the previous story utilized all three forms of communication to get his message across to me. Clairvoyance, clairaudience and clairsentience combined to help free a man who had died more than eighty years before but simply had not realized it.

Chapter 8
PRAYERS, MIRACLES AND HEALING

When I was a younger adult, I prayed to God for things—not material things, just love, happiness and a long, fulfilled life for those I loved. Today I simply say, "Thank you, God," and I say this knowing that whatever occurs does so for a reason. I give thanks for all the good, the less than good, the challenging and the gifts that are bestowed upon me. We often refer to the not-so-good experiences we have as bad. This is a human term that relates to what we have experienced and also involves a judgment of sorts. By not thanking God for the so-called bad in your life, you are missing the bigger picture. Every experience you have ever had, right down to the smallest detail, helps to make you who you are. By simply saying thank you and truly meaning it, you show your faith in God, life and yourself. Then your life is limitless.

I often wonder why, when things are going well, we sail along content, happy and full of hope. At these times, most people never think to say, "Thank you, God," or to even to acknowledge Him and appreciate the fact that they are happy. As soon as one of those life lessons come along, however, we have no difficulty complaining to God, and our first questions are usually, "Why me? Why them? Why not one more day? God, how could you do this to me? What have I done to deserve this?" We think it is as if God is responsible for the bad in our lives. I do not believe God is expecting to hear, "Thanks, you're the greatest." I do not believe God is demanding, and I do not believe that God grants some hopes, dreams and prayers and says no to others. We create our own lives, however they play out. We choose the things we want to experience, and we're given the tools to play this game. The outcome is ours and ours alone. God gave us free will, and I believe Got wants us to use it. There is no bad decision, because bad is relative to us, not God. God exists in two worlds, the absolute (Heaven) and our world of relativity (physical). Why would God give us free choice and then condemn us for using it? The answer is that God doesn't. We need to humanize God, so we give God the qualities we're accustomed to. We make God's love conditional, we see God as judgmental and perhaps worst of all we believe God to be condemning. As a result, we never completely enjoy the full glory of God's love and the opportunities awaiting us. Giving thanks for all things and truly meaning it is one of the first steps to knowing God. Accepting responsibility for our lives and creating what we want to experience is our gift.

I would not presume to tell people how to pray or even that they should pray; this is still part of our free will. Pray or don't pray, do what is right for you and also remember that what is right for you is not necessarily right for anyone else. Afford others the same free will that God has bestowed on all of us. He does not judge and condemn; neither should we. Even knowing this, on occasion I still find myself standing in judgment and ready to condemn. The big difference now is that when this happens, I become aware of what I'm doing and alter my thought processes.

What Is Meant to Be, Will Be

If you pray for direction or for changes to take place in your life, make sure you are perfectly clear in what you are asking for and then watch for the signs. In the past I asked for a way out of a certain situation, and even though I believed with all my heart that what I asked would come to pass, I found that I was not aware of the change even when it landed on my doorstep. For instance, back in 1998 I was trying to stop running a retail store, which I had opened in 1995. Spiritually my heart was now elsewhere, and I asked God for a way out. Three days later, an acquaintance came into the store and asked if I was interested in getting back into the newspaper industry. "Absolutely not," was my reply; I did not even have to think about it. He kept talking to me about the position that was available at a military newspaper. He told me the position was his and that after nine and half years, he was moving on. I admit hearing it was his position being offered to me was somewhat enticing, because my first job in the newspaper industry years earlier had been another position he had decided to leave. He asked me to call him in the next day or so if I changed my mind. After he left, I sat contemplating his offer and wondering how I could possibly take it. I was running my own store and had sworn never to get back into the newspaper business again. When it finally hit me that this was my way out, I am sure Grey Owl had a good laugh. The month before I had hired a friend's daughter to work for me. She was available and willing to work all the hours I could give her. I knew that because this new position was a government newspaper, the stress and demanding nature of the industry would be minimal if it existed at all. In addition, the paper employed only three people (including the available position) and offered a regular pay cheque, benefits and weekends off. What was I thinking when I said no?

I called my acquaintance and told him I had changed my mind and went for an interview, wanting very much to get this job. As I parked my car, Grey Owl told me the only way I would not get it was if I chose not to take it. The interview went extremely well, and the company offered me the position as Grey Owl said it would be. I worked there for over five years and I often thank God for delivering my way out when I needed it. The moral of this story is be careful what you ask for because you will likely get it, and once you have asked, be sure to see the signs and not let an opportunity pass you by. Most of all don't let fear run your life. Live your life from the heart, and it will be an incredible journey.

Healing

Every Wednesday evening, when our small meditation group would gather, we would close the evening with a healing circle. Each of us would write down the names of people who could use healing. The recipients whose names were written down were physically unwell or perhaps going through difficult times. No matter the reason, their names were put into the healing pot. What that person was meant to experience or which path she or he would take remained a personal choice; our wishes and desires played no part in the healing.

First I would like to explain a little of what we do during the healing circle. The lists of names are put into the healing bowl, and when we are ready to begin, we ignite the pieces of paper. At that time I visualize God's white light entering through my crown chakra. I feel this energy course through my body and out my hands, which are stretched out, palms open toward the flame. I can visualize this energy blending with the smoke and rising upward to meet with the Universal Energy (God). At the same time, I pray for the highest and best for those in the healing pot. There are many nights that my guides will instruct me to add names of people, some of whom I don't even know. I always put them in without question.

One night stands out as proof that our healing not only works but adds much to the other person's well-being. On this particular evening, I thought I had written down all the names for the healing bowl. Then Grey Owl instructed me to write the following: "The elderly gentleman on the ground floor of Stevenson Memorial Hospital." No name came through, only the location of this person, and I wrote it down as I was instructed. Stevenson Memorial Hospital is a small rural community hospital of about forty beds; only a very small number of deaths occur here each year. On our drive home that night, I talked to my wife about the message I had received and that I had added him to the healing. Since my wife worked at the hospital, I asked if she would be able to verify whether an older male patient had passed away that evening. I told her I had a strong feeling that something strange and powerful had occurred during our healing .

The next morning Kim called me from work to say that no one had passed in the night. But later that afternoon, Kim called back to say things had changed. She received a phone message from the floor nurse that a patient's chart was on the main floor. This chart belonged to an elderly male patient who had expired at 11:43 the night before. The chart should have come down to Kim's desk first thing in the morning, but for some reason it had not. According to the nurses' notes, although this gentleman was ready to die, from 6:00 p.m. until 9:30 p.m. he was very restless. Shortly after 9:30 p.m. he quieted down and rested peacefully. Our healing took place at 9:30 that evening, and we had all left for home by 10:00 p.m. Some of you may feel this is a coincidence, and some may think I am reaching to make a connection. I believe that all of us in attendance that night helped a fellow human being in his final hours of life. Nothing compares to knowing in my heart and soul that the spirit world will help every one of us, whenever we need them to.

Miracles Do Happen

One of the most dramatic healing circles that our group underwent was a Wednesday night in August 1999. There were five of us present, and that night all of us experienced an incredible healing. The evening progressed typically until one of our members, Wilma, arrived to inform us that her sister was going to have emergency surgery that night. Wilma's sister, Elizabeth Hazel, was in a race for her life with cancer. The primary site was in her bowels but she also had a tumour on her liver. Along with the cancer she was now suffering from a bowel blockage, causing her excruciating pain. The doctors decided that they would cut out the blockage and the tumour and hopefully reconnect the bowel. The worst-case scenario was that she would have to have a colostomy for the rest of her life. One month earlier, the doctors told her the cancer was too advanced and that surgery was not an option. As our group started the healing circle, we focused our attention on this woman that four of us had never met. We sent her pure love and healing energy directed from God and I kept seeing her lying in her hospital bed covered in a pink light with rose petals falling all over her. The energy and the overwhelming sense of peace in the room with us was indescribable. During the twenty-minute healing session, several angels assisted us, and one in particular made his presence known to me. In the centre of our circle, a being of pure light stood in front of us. At first I wasn't sure who he was, and then the answer came to me. As unbelievable as it may sound, this light told me he was Christ. His was such a strong energy, filled with a wonderful enveloping feeling of love, and I was rendered speechless. He walked toward me and placed his hands on my forehead, held them there for a minute and then made his way around the circle doing the same hands-on healing to the other four healers. At the conclusion of the healing, we all discussed what an incredible experience we'd just had. None of us knew just how miraculous it really was. I told the group I had seen Elizabeth in her hospital bed with two women and one man from spirit, all standing at the head of her bed. Then I told them of the visit from Christ. I stated that I wasn't for sure that it was Christ, only that that was who He told me He was. I then tried to put into words the love I felt coming from him was like nothing I had ever experienced before.

At the time it was hard to believe that Christ had visited us. I think I was embarrassed to say that Christ had actually been in the room, because how dared I believe that Jesus Christ Himself came to visit and extend healing to us. You may be thinking the same thing, but all I can tell you is the outcome of that night. The following Monday night my phone rang. It was Wilma, and I sensed she was calling with good news. She began by telling me how her sister was doing, and then she went on to say the most incredible thing had happened that past Wednesday night. Her sister never had the surgery. The doctors decided that before they opened her up, they would do one more check to make certain of the procedure required. They performed a test where a microscopic camera was put into her colon. What they found was astounding. The blockage that had been there the day before had totally disappeared. The tumour had been reduced to a speck in size. The doctors had no explanation. Elizabeth told the doctors what we had done that night, and the doctor told her that we should continue.

Laying on of Hands

I believe anyone can give healing; all that is needed is a desire to help and the intent to heal. You still have to remember, however, that the outcome may be very different from what you were hoping. It is not for us to say that healing an ailment is in the person's highest interest. We do not know what process that person has agreed to experience. Therefore it is best to give healing with the knowledge that your desire and intent are for the highest and best result, even though you do not know what that result will be. I have found that one of the most effective methods of healing is the laying on of hands.

One particular experience stands out in my mind: it involved one of my co-workers, who had constant and crippling migraines. Margrit arrived at work one Friday morning looking to be in a great deal of pain. I cannot relate to the ongoing pain and agony that people have to endure with chronic migraines.

By lunchtime her headache had increased to an unbearable level. It was at this time, while at the local gym for my daily workout, that I received the message to lay my hands on Margrit for the purpose of healing. I was not comfortable with this request because I was not sure how Margrit would take to it. But on returning to work and watching her suffer while trying to finish her day's work so she could leave, I asked if she would like me to give her healing.

She questioned what was involved, and I told her I would lay my hands on her shoulders and let the spirit world do the rest. I also told her I had never done anything like this before, so I did not know exactly what would happen. Her reply was, "Oh yes please, do it."

I stood behind her, put my hands on her shoulders and closed my eyes. I focused my attention on the white light that was flowing down through myself and into Margrit. I was breathing in the white light and passing the healing energy on to her. After about a minute of this, Margrit's father from spirit came in and put his hands on either side of her head. As he did this, her aunt, also from spirit, appeared and held her right arm. I asked Margrit if she was feeling anything different, and she replied in an excited tone that she was. I told her I would let her know what had happened when this was finished, and then I turned my attention to her chakra system. With each breath in, I visualized each centre opening and the energy moving up the many levels of her physical body. After about twelve minutes of this magnificent healing, we were done. Her father and aunt withdrew, and I sat back and asked how she felt. She told me that the pain had gone completely, that the most incredible feeling had passed through her and that her condition changed instantly. I told Margrit about her father and aunt coming to help her, and I said I was also surprised at how quickly and completely the pain had been removed. Margrit was able to continue on for the next two and a half hours and finish her day at work. She thanked me and looked over her right shoulder at me every now and again to mutter, "I can't believe it." I told her that it wasn't me; I was merely the conduit for the healing energy.

Healing comes in many forms—it can be a medical treatment, Reiki, therapeutic touch or the laying on of hands. It can be performed with prayer, and it can come about by simply helping someone. What I do as a medium helps and heals on an emotional level. When a person is healed emotionally, then the physical healing can take place. Regardless of the type of healing you practice, it all begins with intent. Not only is this true in healing but in every word, thought and deed. Intent is at the root of everything we say, do or desire. Know your intent, and you will never be surprised by the outcome of your choices, thoughts and actions.

In this chapter I have given personal examples of the power of prayer and the wonderful healing and calming effect it can have on the person praying as well as the intended recipients. To be able to give unconditional thanks during prayer is truly a life-changing act. Prayers bring joy, calm and love into life and can truly heal all wrongs.

Chapter 9
SUICIDES

Most adults have lost someone close to them. One aspect of death that causes mixed emotions is suicide. Everyone has an opinion, whether it is based in religion or personal, and the opinions can vary drastically.

My personal experiences show me that those who commit suicide do not go to hell, they do not spend time in purgatory and they do not cease to exist. From childhood, I had been taught that suicide was one of the ultimate sins—the sinner's soul would go to hell. I'm sure this came from my limited religious exposure as well as from discussions and hearing others talk about suicide. My heart went out to people who had committed this ultimate sin, because as much as I did not want to believe it, I was sure they were roasting in a fiery pit. Now I laugh at the lengths we will go to create a vengeful and judgmental God.

Suicide evokes strong, negative emotions. If someone loses a family member through natural causes, it is a shock and painful, but it was obviously meant to be—at least that is what we think. We say it must be God's will. If we lose someone through suicide, however, a new twist is added to the mix. There can be shame, guilt, embarrassment and a need for secrecy. We take what that person did very personally, and we struggle to understand what they were thinking. We can't know the pain the person was feeling, and instead the focus of our concern turns to what people will think and the need to protect the person's memory and the family.

If you believe that losing someone through an accident is God's will and that suicide occurs against God's will, you might want to rethink your beliefs. I do not believe in accidents; I believe God's will is our will and our will is Gods. Free will surrounds us; everything in life is a choice, and there are no bad choices. Regardless of the choices we make, the outcome will be the same. We need to understand and know:

> We are all one. We are not separate.
> There is no place to go because we are already there.
> We are one with God.

These messages and more have been shared with the world many times. This particular phrasing comes from Neale Donald Walsch's book, *A Friendship with God*.

How many times have you made a "bad" choice only to discover that everything worked out fine anyway, or you learned something valuable from that choice and the circumstances surrounding it? When someone commits suicide, it is hard to imagine anything good can come of it, but what if through their final act that person helped you in some way? Consider the following scenario: The child who committed suicide was your favourite, and you were not close to your other child. As a result of your loss, you were able to heal and nourish your relationship with that other child. After years of healing and reflection, you could look back and see the beauty of how it all unfolded, even though you would always miss the child who now walks in spirit. It is important to understand that the beauty lies not in the child's death but as a result of it. All is perfect, especially at those times when life seems anything but perfect.

God addresses suicide in Neale Donald Walsch's *Conversations with God, Book 3* and explains that suicide is a matter of perspective and time. The act of putting a gun to one's head and pulling the trigger is suicide; however, smoking for thirty-five years, or drinking excessively all of one's life, would be considered commerce. God asks that we consider the difference—it is the amount of time it takes to kill the body. We are conditioned to look at events as if one is better or more acceptable than another, however both choices will result in the same outcome. One will just take longer.

Losing a Child to Suicide

I believe that losing a child is the most painful experience anyone will ever have to face. This profound loss can be further compounded if that child committed suicide. I cannot begin to understand the level of pain, loss and emptiness that parents feel at this time, but I do receive glimpses. I also experience the heartfelt emotions from those in the spirit world, and that is as close as I ever want to come. As the father of four beautiful children, my heart goes out to everyone who has or will endure this kind of loss.

A Friendship Rekindled Just in Time

I have never contemplated suicide, but it has impacted on my life more than once. The event that most touched my heart was the death of a good friend, Brian. Brian was a person with a huge heart and a great sense of humour. In fact, the only thing average about Brian was his height. The first time I met him, I saw a long-haired, tattooed, cigarette-smoking hippie. I categorized him immediately and realized Brian experienced this form of judgment every day of his adult life. His hard outer shell did a great job of hiding the wonderful person he was on the inside. Brian had many good qualities, and he could always find ways to turn negative situations into positive ones. He was a natural-born salesman with the gift of communication. He connected easily with people, and I often watched amazed as he conversed with ministers and bikers and anyone in between. Our friendship developed quickly, and I could relate to him easily.

It was his ability to sell that first brought us together in the business world. I offered him a job at the small newspaper I was running. He liked the idea and jumped at the opportunity. When I introduced him to the people at our head office in another town, I asked them not to judge a book by its cover. They agreed to wait and see the results. Brian never let any of us down, and he brought so much humour into our tiny office that going to work became fun once again.

After a few months of working together and socializing outside of work, Brian broached the possibility of our starting a new business together. I have to admit I was keen on getting out of the newspaper industry, and this seemed like a good idea to me. Brian suggested an adult novelty store, and although I liked the idea, I didn't really think it was feasible. When I told my wife our new idea, she asked if I was crazy. She didn't wait for my response she simply and forcefully said, "No way!" For some twisted reason, this spurred me on, and after months of planning, researching and location hunting, we were finally ready to put our plan into action. It took a year for my wife to become comfortable with the idea of an adult store. Her biggest concern was what people would think. My wife is a great person, and I don't say that because she eventually gave her blessing. I think the reason behind her relenting speaks volumes. Years later, after it was all said and done, she told me she knew it wasn't right, but the only way for me to discover this would be to do what I wanted. She has always supported me even when she knew it would not turn out well.

Once we opened our store, it didn't take me long to realize that with Brian, the planning of the business, telling people what we were doing and the status that it somehow created for him was the drawing card. But once the ball started rolling, he seemed to lose interest. Five short weeks after our doors opened, I knew I could not take it any longer. Our friendship had taken three years to build and just two months to destroy. I wanted to buy Brian's share, but when his wife refused the offer, in August 1995 I agreed they could buy me out. After the arguments and hurt feelings, I felt that we finally parted amicably, and I truly wished him the best. I know he felt the same for me. No one person was to blame for the breakup of both our business and friendship, but it was a very uncomfortable situation. What had brought Brian and I together as friends ultimately divided us.

In October 1995, I opened my new store in a different town. I carried on as if nothing had happened, but the way things had turned out continued to eat away at me. A year and a half passed before I saw Brian again. He came into my store on Remembrance Day 1996. We talked for about twenty minutes and then he left. Another eighteen months went by before my next contact. Late in January 1998, his mother, Bernie, called to tell me that Brian was in bad shape. She said he had lost weight and seemed very unhappy; he had even started drinking again. Brian was an alcoholic and had been sober for more than ten years. I told her to let me know if there was anything I could do to help, and I meant it. I asked her to relay to Brian that if he wanted to talk, he only had to call. I had always regretted the void left where our friendship had been.

When no call had come in over a week, I contacted his mother to see if things had improved. She told me that he would be calling; he was just in an emotional slump at this time. I finally heard from him late one night in February. We talked for two hours, and I could tell he wasn't the Brian I remembered. He had heard through the grapevine that I had undergone a drastic change, and he wanted to know exactly what I was doing. He was referring to my mediumship, and I told him what had happened and how my gift came about. I also told him not to worry if he had trouble believing this, because he would simply be one of many. He said that, having heard it from me, he believed.

He had a lot of questions that night about what I did as well as what life after death was really like. I told him what I could, and I believe it helped him. He told me about his problems, his frame of mind and what had transpired in his life over the past ten months. He touched on his nervous breakdown, weight loss and paranoia. The breakdown of his marriage shocked me because I knew how much Brian loved his wife. At the end of our conversation, I told Brian I would come to see him in the next couple of days. I felt so good that night; after almost three years we had talked and put all that senseless garbage behind us.

Two days later I went to his house and could scarcely believe my eyes when he opened the door. My friend had been very healthy looking, but the man who stood in front of me now was little more than skin and bones. I walked in trying to hide my surprise, but just as on our first meeting years earlier, he knew what I was thinking. We talked for an hour about Brian's condition, his marriage and a vision that played itself out over and over in his head. He told me that he saw himself sitting on his couch watching television when time seemed to stop. In front of him he watched as a movie began playing out. This movie wasn't on television—he was in it. He saw himself walk over to the closet, pull out a shotgun and return to the couch. He described in detail how he sat there with tears streaming down his face and pulled the trigger. As soon as the gun went off, he snapped back to reality. It scared him enormously to contemplate such an act.

He assured me that after this incident he had taken all of his guns to his father's house and left them there under lock and key. I asked him to promise that there were no guns in his house. I stayed and talked to him for another hour and from that day on agreed to remain in touch. Numerous times I invited him to visit, and Brian always agreed but never arrived.

During the latter part of April, Brian called to say things had not improved. Oddly enough, our friendship was as solid as it had ever been. The following day he stopped at my store for the first time since November 1996. He came into my back office and sat down while I poured him a coffee. As I sat with him, he broke down and began to cry. I tried for an hour to console him, to let him know that I was there for him no matter what. He was physically wasted and very tired, a shell of the man I had known. I sat wondering how this could have happened. While we talked about his problems, I saw a male and a female spirit standing beside him. I described the man and told Brian that he was showing me a large incision on his chest. I told him this man was

an uncle and had passed from cancer. Brian confirmed that it was his uncle.
I cannot remember what other messages, if any, were received that day, but
I tried to convince Brian that everything would be fine. I could not have
been more wrong. The last time I saw Brian alive was three weeks before
his death. I stopped at his place of work to invite him over for the evening.
He accepted but never arrived.

Before that evening, whenever I had visited Brian's mother, she would ask
if I sensed anything about Brian. The only thing I was being told was that
he and his wife would not divorce. At this time, his family's concern was
focused more on the marriage. I was never shown that within a week's time,
my friend would be dead, and I certainly wasn't shown that he would take
his own life.

On Friday, May 8, 1998, I had just finished dinner when the phone rang.
It was Bernie, Brian's mother, calling with the dreadful news. Brian had
shot himself!

"Oh Bernie, I am so very sorry," I said in shock and disbelief.

I asked how everyone was, although I could imagine only too well. She just
kept repeating over and over, "He has done it, he has really done it!" I went
to her home that night unsure of what I would say or what I could do, but
I had to go. On my way there a tape was playing in my car, and the first
song to come on was "Remember Me" by Sarah McLachlan. The words
in this song were so poignant that as I drove, tears filled my eyes. I knew
Brian was okay and that he was in a better place, but my heart went out to
his family, and I cried because my friend was gone. I knew that two hours
earlier a horrendous event had taken place, and this family would never be
the same again. I wanted them to know that I cared.

Brian's funeral was held the following Monday; his remains had already
been cremated. At the front of the church were bouquets of flowers, an
older picture of Brian showing him with a full beard and moustache and

an urn holding his ashes. The service started, and his brother-in-law gave the eulogy. Throughout the service I tried to see if Brian was present. I was not getting anything, but this did not surprise me because my ability seldom works for my own benefit. When we were asked to pray, however, I closed my eyes, and there in front of me stood my friend with a smile on his face, white light flowing from behind and illuminating his body. Despite my childhood thoughts and fears about suicide, I knew with complete certainty he was in a safe and happy place.

Brian stayed with me for quite some time during the service and even showed he had retained his sense of humour. During the service the minister asked us to sing a couple of hymns. The thought of me singing in public could be considered cruel to the people congregated there. However, Brian stood before me once again, laughing loudly and telling me to sing. He thought it would be funny. His joy flooded over me, and I had to control the smile that threatened to spread from ear to ear. The happiness that filled me could not be contained as he continued to be unrelenting about my singing. I finally agreed and began to sing softly at first, then louder and stronger as the hymn went on. Brian was laughing heartily at my level of discomfort; he knew I could not carry a tune.

I think it is wonderful that at such a sad time for his family and friends, Brian could find humour in his funeral. I know he was deeply concerned for his family, but he said "I'm okay." I told Kim what was going on during the service, but I waited a couple of weeks before talking to Brian's mother. I could only imagine the heartache she was going through, and I knew she was not ready to hear what I had to tell her. When I did visit her, she confided that her worse fear was of Brian being in hell because of committing suicide. This was my opportunity to tell her what I had seen and experienced. I reassured her that Brian was in a better place and that he was whole, complete and full of laughter. I do not know how much she believed because I think a lot of what I said fell on deaf ears. Although my friend has come to visit me only a handful of times in the years since he passed over, his visits are a welcomed comfort.

As I write this, my friend has joined me from the spirit world. His energy sweeps through my body, and he stands tall behind my left shoulder, his hearty laugh echoing loud above me. I ask Brian if there is anything he would like to inject into my writing. He laughs at my choice of words and says, "Life is full of magical, mystical events. To not cherish each and every one of them is a crime against who you really are."

When I ask Brian if he has any regrets, he replies, "How can you regret a perfect world?" He wants us to know he can now see the grander vision of life and is extremely thankful that he can appreciate what he had and has. His concern is centred on those left behind, although he knows peace and solace will come to them also. His actions were based on what he knew and how he assessed his life at that time. He is beside those who grieve and comforts them when they need it. As in life, his family remains his main concern. The "what if" game is pointless; he would like his family to get on with their lives. He has not left their side.

A Mother Finds Forgiveness

A client named David was a middle-aged man who had first come to me for an appointment seven months earlier. That night had stayed in my mind. Because he lived two hours away, I had pressured myself to be accurate and perform to the best of my abilities so his trip would not be in vain. The spirit world has never let me down, but my ego said, "You just never know." As I walked out to meet him and his companion that day, I slid a wooden block between the doorframe and the self-locking door. After we made our introductions and turned to go in, the door closed behind me. My keys were inside lying on my desk, and I had no way of getting in. Embarrassment washed over me, and I found myself apologizing over and over. At that time, I conducted my appointments at my place of work, so although I knew there were others who worked in the building with keys, I had no idea where to find them on a weeknight. David drove me to a phone booth where I began my frantic search for someone to open the door. I know that Grey Owl and Gabriel had a good laugh at my misadventure. Looking back, I realize that this new worry completely removed the pressure about the session. Once we finally got in, the reading was incredible for David and his friend, Linda.

Now David was returning for another appointment for himself and friends. I do not advertise my services, so anyone who finds their way to me does so by word of mouth. I was pleased that David thought enough of my ability to return with friends. When his car pulled up, I went out to meet him, and this time I made sure my keys were safely in my hand. There were three people with him: Carol, Travis and Vicky, and all greeted me with hellos and warm smiles. Vicky seemed very quiet and somewhat nervous. After the exchange of pleasantries, the reading began.

The first person to come through was Carol's cousin. This lady described her fight with cancer, talked of her feelings about passing and repeatedly told Carol that she was fine and extremely happy. Carol told me that her cousin had just passed the month before, and though she was happy to hear from her, this was not the message she was hoping to receive. The next person to come through was Carol's daughter, Jenna. I felt there had been a suicide around her, and although I could not pinpoint the cause of death, all I could get was that asphyxiation was involved.

"That is correct," she said.

"Now I'm seeing that there are two deaths around you. There is one death, and then a little time passes, and there is a second death, a suicide. There is an illness involved with one of the deaths as well."

"'That is right, you're correct with all that," she said.

Next, Jenna talked to her mother, and her brother, Travis, Jenna said she was sorry for what she had done to them, but she was doing everything she could to help them cope. Jenna was a good communicator who gave me undeniable personality traits, phrases and accounts of her life to prove to her mother that she was in fact okay. Jenna explained she had not thought straight a lot of the time. She talked of an illness in her head and again apologized. She also said she was not alone at the time of her death. Throughout the reading, Jenna told her mom several times that at Christmas she was to ring a bell.

Although Carol was happy that Jenna had made contact, I could sense there was still someone else from which she was waiting to hear. As Jenna stood next to her mother and caressed her shoulder, a little girl walked forward and grabbed Jenna's left hand. This beautiful, smiling angel, with her hair shimmering over her tiny form, stood silently for a moment and then said, "I am three years old." Carol burst into tears and sobbed uncontrollably. I told Carol this little girl was very happy.

Then everything became clear for me. "Did Jenna take her young daughter's life and then commit suicide?" I asked. Through her tears Carol nodded yes!

After a few moments of silence, Carol spoke again. "I am so happy she is with her mother, but I am surprised that she would be. I am very sorry to have lost a daughter and a granddaughter as well; that is a lot to handle."

Carol's granddaughter continued showing me that when she was found, people hooked up IVs and tried getting oxygen into her tiny body, but it wasn't meant to be.

"Carol, it is important that you know they are both doing well, and your granddaughter is very happy," I reassured her.

The reading ended shortly after this, and Carol told me that it had brought peace and some happiness to her, knowing they both were fine, but she still had a lot of work to do as far as her emotions and forgiveness were concerned. She also told me some of the circumstances of that awful day: how Jenna had taken the life of her three-year-old daughter and then barricaded herself in her room and taken her own life a few hours later. A friend of Jenna's had been unsuccessful in her attempts to break into the room. Carol thanked me repeatedly for what I had done, and I felt good knowing I had been instrumental in helping her find some much-needed peace. Although I could not provide her with complete closure, I was able to help Carol and her family start down the road of healing and forgiveness. For that I am extremely grateful.

Sympathetic Pain

I have already talked about how I receive the messages, but I have not discussed the process of sympathetic pain. On occasion, I will take on the pain of the person from spirit. This can be extremely uncomfortable and somewhat frightening. The most vivid account of sympathetic pain I can remember was with a client called Kerry. She had booked an appointment with me for a Sunday, and like David, she also had a two-hour drive to reach me. What made Kerry's story different was that for the week leading up to our meeting, I knew of one spirit who eagerly awaited this reading. As soon as Kerry sat down, I was overcome with anticipation and anxiety. I told her I felt there was a male wanting to make contact and that he had committed suicide. With a look of surprise, Kerry began to cry.

"I am sorry to upset you, but I have to tell you he has been with me all week; he seems very impatient," I said. Before I could get another word out, my throat closed up, my chest tightened and I felt the most incredible pain around my neck. It caught me so off-guard that I was at a loss for several minutes, and then as quickly as it began, it was over. I regained my composure, caught my breath and then explained to Kerry what had happened. I asked if this man had hung himself. Once again, in surprise, she replied that I was correct.

He showed me the interior of a car, a pill bottle and the fact that he hanged himself in a tree. At the time of the reading she wasn't sure about the pill bottle, but the autopsy indicated he had medication in his blood. I believe sometimes the spirits provide so much information to loved ones that they cannot fully process it all in that moment, and they need time to sort through it.

The session went well, and at its conclusion, Kerry told me what had happened. For reasons still unknown to her, her husband drove out to the spot where they were married, and under the tree where they said their vows, he took his life.

Sometimes answers and reasons are not spelled out clearly, even for those people who are so desperately seeking them. Hopefully Kerry is now on a path of understanding and healing. My prayers go out to her.

I am not minimizing the pain of those who have experienced a loss to suicide, and I am not making a judgment regarding suicide; I am simply providing another perspective for your consideration. For anyone who has ever lost a loved one from suicide, please take comfort in knowing your beloved will be safe, loved and surrounded and helped by those who went before them. I learned these details firsthand from Brian and the countless others who have delivered messages of love and hope to their families through me.

Chapter 10
MOTHER AND SON REUNITE IN HEAVEN

Life is an amazing process full of highs and lows, shrouded in miracles and interwoven amid tragedies and synchronized events. Over the years I have discovered that time is the key factor, unfolding in amazing perfection. It allows a person to be able to focus on the perfection and ultimate beauty that comes from all tragedy. Like a phoenix rising from the ashes, humans possess the same incredible fortitude to face and ultimately triumph over tragedy. Debbie Ure is that phoenix with a truly remarkable story.

I have been blessed to meet many remarkable and life-changing people through my work. Unbeknown to me, Friday, July 20, 2007, would be one of those days, and Debbie Ure would be one of those life-changing, inspirational figures to leave an indelible mark on my life. Courage comes in many shapes and sizes, but none larger than Debbie exuded.

Muskoka, Ontario, Canada, is Ontario's Garden of Eden and is dotted with majestic, breath-taking, crystal-clear lakes. The area is known as cottage country, the playground for tens of thousands of weekend commuters during the summer months.

That Friday afternoon in 2007, driving to Gravenhurst, a small town in Muskoka, seemed no different than any other time I had taken the drive north. I have travelled that highway my entire life, but today was different. It was the first time that I had been asked to conduct a lecture and demonstration in that area. My lecture was to start at 7:00 p.m., and having never been there for work in the past, I did not know what to expect. Standing in the backroom of the hall, I had prepared myself through meditation and prayer. I could hear the hustle and bustle of the crowd getting settled in their seats from behind the door that separated us. My frame of mind felt great, and as I paced back and forth trying to control the building energy bursting out from me, I could not wait to hit the stage. It truly is remarkable how a guy who was for a great deal of his life paralyzed with fear with the prospect of public speaking now found himself loving and craving the spotlight and connection with whatever crowd was eagerly awaiting him. Now fear and nerves never play a part for me when I am working in large crowds.

From beyond the door I could hear the announcer welcome everyone and give a quick introduction of who I was and what I did. As I opened the door, I took a deep breath and heard Grey Owl speak to me in his gentle tone, "Enjoy tonight," and I smiled. As I entered the hall and walked to the stage, I was aware of a hall filled to almost capacity, and my first thought was, This will be a great night for the two organizations that benefited from the ticket sales that evening.

The first hour was a question–and-answer segment that helped get the audience into the proper frame of mind while providing a basis of fact for those who have never attended a seminar of this nature. Quip after quip, I had the crowd laughing as I shared stories from client readings over the years. After a short intermission, I hit the stage once again. If I was to feel any nerves during a seminar, this was when the serpent of doubt reared its ugly head, and for a split second I thought, What if no one comes through? I focused on the crowd, rubbed my hands together and opened up to receive, and in a sense that is when the magic began.

Trust is a major component of my work, and like a baby bird being tossed out of the nest by its mother; I will either fly or fall hard. Thank God I always seem to soar. Sometimes I soar higher than at other times, but I can honestly say that those in spirit have never let me hit the ground.

Following the first two contacts, I explained to the crowd that I had a young man coming through and was being pulled to the very back of the room. I walked up the centre aisle and stopped halfway back, pointing to the back row on the left side of the hall. I made reference to a young man coming through who talked about a blow to the head. "I know I have a young man with an impact to his head, and his death was swift. Now he is showing me that it took place on or beside a road, and I am seeing rock cuts all around this area." I looked up and asked, "Does anyone in this area understand what is coming through?"

A woman sitting at the end of the row in the aisle I was pointing at raised her hand. I made eye contact and for the first time realized this woman was wearing a back and neck brace. I asked her what she understood that I had said. She said she had the connection with a young male, who passed with a blow to the head on the road. Once she acknowledged the information, the connection was strengthened even more.

This young man was very excited to convey the fact that he was okay and that he had been in this woman's life ever since that tragic day. He called her Mom and said he was safe. This woman was visibly moved by what she heard.

I have learned over the years to not put my spin on the messages as they come through. I had assumed based on the details I was hearing that this woman's son had been killed in a car accident, although that assumption would ultimately be wrong. I did not mention a car accident to her, because her son did not show me a vehicle or any scenario that would indicate a car accident. It was purely my assumption of the facts that at the time led me to believe he had passed as result of a motor vehicle accident.

Validation after validation came through, and tears rolled down her cheek as for the first time in what would have been almost fifteen years, this woman knew her son was okay. At one point in the reading, her son told me to say, "Scooter." I had no clue who or what Scooter was, but what I did know was that this young man had proven himself to be a great communicator. So I said, "He wants me to say Scooter to you." She just about fell out of her chair, and half the audience gasped loudly and in unison.

She wiped tears away and cleared her throat and muttered the word, "That was Wes's dog." Many in the audience knew that detail and were astonished by the fact that Wes sealed the deal for his mother that night by acknowledging the family pet from years before. Wes pulled back after telling his mom he loved her, and the evening ended shortly thereafter.

As I was packing up to leave following the lecture, Wes's mom, Debbie, came up to the stage and wanted to thank me for the messages. We hugged, and she told me that her son had been murdered in 1992. She recounted the story of how on June 29, 1992, her son Wes and his best friend, Santo, were coming home after a weekend at a friend's cottage, and how an act of kindness of picking up a couple of guys hitchhiking on Highway 117 cost her son and his friend their lives.

The two hitchhikers decided to steal Santo's car, but before doing so, they forced the two nineteen-year-old boys out of the car and placed them on their knees in the centre of the road. With one quick pull of the trigger to the back of the head of each of the boys, these two thugs took the lives of two innocent young men, whose only crime was an act of compassion. Debbie told me their shooting spree was not done, and as they were fleeing down the highway, a police officer had stopped the vehicle in the city of Barrie, Ontario, for speeding. The police officer was unaware of the crime the men in the car had committed just forty-five minutes earlier in another town. As he approached the vehicle, the driver pulled a gun and shot the officer three times. Miraculously, she said, the police officer was not killed and somehow survived the execution-style rampage. The two men were apprehended hours later and were sentenced to prison for two counts of first-degree murder and attempted murder of a police officer.

I drove home that night feeling a sense of accomplishment and satisfaction. The evening went well, and I felt some great connections had been made. What I did not know at the time was that I would not be finished with Wes or his mother.

My next encounter with mother and son came eleven months later on May 28, 2008. As a medium I have no previous knowledge of my clients ahead of time, and I do not know who will walk through my office door next. I do not handle scheduling appointments for clients; that is left up to my wife. I prefer it this way for a couple of reasons. I like the fact that I have no previous conversation or awareness of anyone who graces my office door step. The second reason I prefer not having any contact with clients ahead of time is often they share too much personal information about the deceased at the time of scheduling appointments, and I prefer knowing nothing ahead of time.

This particular morning a middle-aged woman opened my office door and walked in. I stood up and walked over to greet her, and as I went to shake her hand and introduce myself, she put out her left hand and shook my right hand as she swayed her right arm and said, "It is just for decoration." It was obvious that she had a crippled arm. She told me her name was Debbie as she took her seat. I had no sense of familiarity or reason to believe we had ever met before.

Once the reading commenced, I had a young man in spirit enter the room from my right side and stood by Debbie's left leg, and he smiled at her. I conveyed this information to her, and she smiled and nodded her understanding. The young man told me he had head trauma and died due to an impact to his head. Once again Debbie nodded her understanding. The reading continued on smoothly for what must have been twenty minutes with validating facts about Debbie, her family and her son in spirit. Then within seconds the tone and mood of the reading changed drastically. Debbie's son uttered words to me to convey to his mother that stopped me in my tracks. I was shocked and, for perhaps one of the few times in my life, was left speechless. This young man looked at me and said, "Tell my mother she is dying and she need not to be afraid; I will be with her every step of the way, and I will be the first person she sees when she crosses over. She will be all right."

Panic washed over me, and I was filled with anxiety. My personal code of ethics and guidelines that I follow when working is that if I hear it, see it or feel it from spirit, I must pass it on to the client. I always believed that the information I receive is not meant for me; it is always and without exception meant for my client. This information her son imparted on me caused me to reconsider my code of ethics.

Debbie could see my distress, and I told her I was sorry for the delay, but I want to check the information I had just received from her son once again. Clearly and strongly her son said yet again, "Tell my mother she is dying and not to be scared; I will be with her." I did not think I would be able to deliver this young man's message; I felt sick and had serious doubts of how clearly I was hearing him.

I asked this young man through my mind if he was sure. I told him that I could not relay his message to his mom. He looked at me and said in the kindest and gentlest way, "You must—she needs to know this."

Debbie could see that I was very uncomfortable with the information I had just received and said, "Just tell me, Chris. I want to know everything." I checked with Grey Owl, my trusted confident, and asked him if I was hearing this young man correctly. Grey Owl simply nodded.

Debbie pleaded with me to tell her what her son had said. I looked at her and took a deep breath. I knew I could not just blurt it out, and with my heart in my throat I slowly began and said, "Debbie, how is your health?"

She grinned and said, "Not too good, I suspect."

A sense of relief washed over me, and I said one of the stupidest things I had ever said to a client, "Oh good, you know then that your health is not good." A huge sense of relief showered me as I said those silly words. I realized how crazy I had just sounded and apologized to her, and Debbie just laughed. I said to her I had something very difficult to tell her, and I was not sure how she would take it. Once again Debbie assured me that she expected only the truth from me and her son.

I took one more deep breath and told her exactly what her son had said to me moments before. I told her she was dying, that her son would be with her and that she should not fear her death. She smiled and, with more grace than I had ever seen before, thanked me. I had just told this woman she was going to die, and she thanked me! What a crazy world we live in, I thought.

Debbie's next words stopped me dead in my tracks yet again. She looked me in the eye and said, "Ask Wes for me when I will die." I looked at her with horror yet again and said, "Only God knows when anyone's moment of death will be, Debbie."

That did not satisfy her need to know, and she asked once again, "Wes will tell me, so ask him, please." I looked at Wes, and he smiled and said to tell her April.

I cleared my throat yet again and relayed the information. With a surprising sense of enthusiasm she said, "My birthday is in April! Ask him if I will die on my birthday, and does he mean next April?" Wes said nothing more. I checked over and over, but he said nothing more on this topic. I assured Debbie that I might have misheard him and that maybe he was referring to her birthday and not her death date. I knew I had heard him correctly but was trying to backpedal for Debbie's sake. The reading came to an end, and I was busting with questions for her that I could not ask during the session. Before I could say anything, Debbie said, "I suspected I was dying, and you have brought me much peace today, Chris. Thank you".

I asked her what her health issue was, because Wes never confirmed any details for us. She started by recounting that I had read her the year before at the Gravenhurst lecture. She told me her son came through and recounted some of the details for me in hopes I would remember. Once she brought up the Scooter, reference I could recall the woman in the back brace and some of the details. Debbie continued to tell me how much comfort she received knowing her son was okay. Then it dawned on me that her son had been murdered, and I said to her, "Wes never alluded to the fact that he was murdered again today."

She said, "No, I guess he did not need to relive that for me."

Debbie then said she had a specialist appointment that afternoon in Toronto that she had no intention of keeping. However now that Wes confirmed what she had suspected, she said she would keep it. She told me that the doctors suspected that she had ALS, better known as Lou Gehrig's disease. My heart sank, and she said she was relieved to know the truth. She also said she would not be scared now that she knew for certain her son would greet her. She told me that her family did not know, and she told them that her partial paralysis was from nerve damage the year before from a car accident. She informed me that was why she was in a back and neck brace at the lecture.

Debbie left and headed off to the city to keep her appointment with the specialist, and she found out what she had been told hours before by her son. She had been handed a death sentence.

I saw Debbie on two other occasions over the next year. One was at another lecture in her home town, and the second was at a workshop I conducted the next fall. Each time I saw Debbie, her conditioned had deteriorated, and by that fall she was confined to a wheelchair. Her spunky personality and her humour were always evident to me at those encounters.

The end of March 2010 was fast approaching, and late on a Tuesday afternoon the phone rang. As usual, Kim answered the call, suspecting it was in all likelihood a client calling. Moments later she emerged from the kitchen with tears in her eyes and said, "You need to talk to this woman; it is about Debbie from Gravenhurst." Kim handed me the phone and I said, "Hello?"

A woman's voice from the other end, said, "Hello, my name is Susan, and I am a coordinator with the ALS organization. I am calling on behalf of Deborah Ure. Deborah can barely speak and has requested I call you, Chris, to ask for a reading with you by phone, and it would have to take place before next Friday, April 2."

I asked her what the urgency was and stated that I was completely booked up and would not be able to accommodate a phone reading that next week. Susan told me that next Friday was Debbie's birthday and that she had decided to have her feeding tube removed that day and take matters into her own hands. Upon hearing that detail, my mind flashed back to her reading almost two years, earlier when Wes had told his mom she would cross over in April.

I swallowed hard and told Susan I was not comfortable with doing Debbie's final reading over the phone. I thumbed through my calendar looking for some possibility and then suggested that if it was all right with Debbie, I would prefer to visit her in person and conduct the reading face to face. It simply did not feel appropriate to honour her final request over the phone. Susan told me that Debbie just smiled, started crying and uttered the words, "I would be honoured." I suggested that I could come up the following Tuesday, March, 30, late in the afternoon following my daytime office appointments. So it was set that the next Tuesday I would drive to Debbie's home over an hour away and hopefully convey messages of hope and inspiration to comfort her in her final days.

That Tuesday arrived and after concluding my in-office readings , I headed up the highway back to Gravenhurst. During the drive, my mind raced with details of who might come through, what might be said and the sombre reality of importance for this reading. Just before I arrived at Debbie's home, a visitor joined me in the car. Wes could not or did not wait for me to arrive at his mom's to start to convey messages for her.

Wes wanted me to tell his mom that he would be the first person she would see upon her transition to the other side. He also wanted her to know they would be running in a field filled with butterflies floating all around them. Perhaps the thing he was most excited about was the fact that his mom would finally find forgiveness for herself when she crossed, something he said she had never been able to find in life.

I arrived at Debbie's house shortly before 4:00 p.m., and as I was about to knock on the door, I noticed a taped sign that read, "No tears are allowed in here, with the exception for Debbie. If you cry, your parking permit will not be validated." I laughed and thought how wonderful it was that she still retained her sense of humour. Upon knocking I could hear what sounded like two very small, yappy dogs barking. Anyone who knows me knows I am not a fan of small dogs.

Upon entering I could see Debbie lying in her hospital bed in the living room, which had been converted into a bedroom. I walked in and saw a tinier version of the Debbie I remembered seeing the year before. Present with Debbie were her nurse, Suzanne, and her friend and confident, Lynn. She smiled and said, "I'm not afraid to die."

After a few minutes of small talk, which provided me time to adjust to the reality of what was taking place, I was ready to begin the reading.

I took a few deep breaths and started by informing Debbie that we had three people from spirit joining us. I had Wes standing next to my left side, beside the hospital bed. I also had a mom or mother figure coming through and an older male that would be a father figure.

I gave Debbie the details. Wes was anxious for her to know what he had recited to me in the car on the way up that afternoon. After recounting all that I could remember, Debbie became very emotional. The most significant impact on her was Wes' last message about her truly being able to find forgiveness for herself following her physical death.

Wes then asked his mom to do him a favour. He stated, "Before your feeding tube is removed, before the last of your nourishment ceases, I want you to close your eyes and visualize yourself eating a piece of your birthday cake." Debbie laughed and groaned. Wes also warned his mom not to get crusty with people and to not kick them out the room in the coming days. Again she laughed. He acknowledged that as much as she wanted people around, sometimes she wanted to just be left alone, and she will have to watch how she expressed herself.

Wes then said, "Mom I made you a promise two years ago in your reading" (and at that point he laughed and said he knew how difficult it was for me to convey the message to his mom years earlier) "and I'm going to deliver on it." That promise was that he would help cross her over, and he would be there to greet her when she crossed over. Then he added, "Mom, I am standing by my word." Debbie cried harder.

I then asked Debbie if she knew of a Jeff connection to Wes, to which she nodded yes. Wes talked about his two brothers and said, "One is having great trouble accepting what is happening to you, and he will continue to have difficulty accepting your choice and your death, but I am helping him the best he can to accept what is."

Debbie raised her left arm off the bed and asked where Wes was standing. My response was, "Right here, Debbie, he is standing right to my left side next to the bed, and I have a woman standing next to the Kleenex box."

Debbie asked, "Can he touch me?"

My reply was, "If he wants to, he can; I am sure he has been around you a lot. Debbie, he wants you to know in the remaining days, do not try to feel for him with your body, but feel for him with your heart".

Wes and the older female stated how every night one of the two dogs Debbie owned slept with her curled up on her right side on the bed, and the other dog never came up. Debbie and her nurse and friend Lynn laughed at this detail and quickly confirmed it.

Wes made mention of how his mother had looked after all details of her life and death, and he laughed saying "It is because she has control issues, and she does not want it screwed up."

Debbie struggled for breath and words and said, "I know."

Wes said, "You are a fighter, and great fighters never quit, but they do know when to walk away. And again you are taking control of this the best way you can. We want you to know we are very proud of you, so very proud of you."

I continued conveying their messages to Debbie. "There is one word they don't want you speaking or thinking, Debbie, and that word is sorry. You do not need to feel sorry for anything. You do not need to tell anyone you are sorry, because it takes away a little bit of who you are each time you say it."

Debbie fought to clear her throat.

I brought Wes's next thoughts through to his mom. "This might sound morbid, but when it is all said and done, the plans you have set up for yourself include no one being able to look at you after, is that correct? That is what Wes is telling me."

Debbie smirked and said, "Yep!" Debbie's stubbornness was ever present. She cleared her throat and fought to get the words out. "Ask Wes when I will die."

I looked at her and laughed a nervous laugh, asking, "Was it not enough that he told you April two years ago?"

She looked at me and stated, "He will tell you, and I want to know."

I waited for Wes's response, and he said, "Tell her the seventh.". I looked at Debbie and then at her nurse Suzanne, and once again just like two years before I backpedalled by stating I could not be sure if what I heard was referring to the date of her transition from this life to the next. I said, "He tells me the seventh." I looked again at Suzanne and asked, "Is that even possible?" Suzanne nodded her head yes. I followed this up by saying I truly didn't know if he meant April 7 or if he meant at 7:00 p.m. I felt uncomfortable and awkward by this whole exchange, and then Debbie thanked me.

Debbie was a fighter and very inspirational to say the least. She looked at me and said, "You know it could be worse."

I laughed out loud and said, "Do tell."

When she replied that she could have cancer and that would be worse, I was overwhelmed by what an inspirational and positive person she was.

After an hour and ten minutes, Debbie's final reading came to an end. I sat and talked with her for a few minutes, squeezing her hand and telling her how much she had impacted me. The impact was remarkable—both professionally and personally—that she and her son had made on my life. I then took the time to ask her how she felt about me including her story and Wes's story in the book I was writing. She smiled a warm smile and nodded and said, "Oh yes." It felt right for me to seek her approval, and I felt blessed when she responded enthusiastically.

I left Debbie's home that day with a lump in my throat, and my heart filled with love and thankfulness knowing that Wes had once again delivered the goods to help his mother in her final days. A sense of accomplishment washed over me as I drove out of her driveway. My thoughts were with Debbie over the next several days, and often I wondered how her struggle was going.

That next week passed quickly, and on Wednesday, April 7, I was checking my e-mail account in between appointments when I noticed a new e-mail with Deborah Ure as the subject title. The message was sent from Suzanne, her nurse, at 11 a.m. that morning letting me know that Deborah had passed on April 7, 2010.

My first thought was, Wow, Wes the little bugger was correct again. I sat there dazed and overwhelmed by the fact that Wes knew two years earlier that his mother would pass in April and then to pin the exact date. I responded to Suzanne's e-mail by thanking her and telling her to take comfort in knowing Debbie was now running in that field with her son . I received an additional phone call that evening from Debbie's friend, Lynn, also telling me Debbie had passed that morning at four minutes to seven.

Through the years I have experienced many incredible, and at times hard to believe, situations as a medium. This one truly was in my top three. During my last visit with Debbie, we both had agreed on a sign that she would provide me from spirit to prove it was her coming through to me. I will keep that sign a secret for now, but I know one day, whether I get it directly from her or perhaps through another medium, Debbie will make good on her promise to let me know it is her.

Debbie's story is truly remarkable for many reasons. Her ability to survive the murder of her nineteen-year-old son as well as her bravery in facing a death sentence with ALS is inspirational to say the least. The fact that her son had acknowledged her impending death to the exact month and later to the day is surreal to me even now. But it does reinforce one simple fact that many of my clients often hear from their deceased loved ones during a session, and that phrase is, "It was my time to die."

Chapter 11
A LESSON LEARNED

Looking back, I see that it was a learning experience. I had been a medium for about two and half years, and although my gift came to me quickly and easily, I was, then as now, continuing to learn about myself with every session.

Some clients had heard about me through a couple that had visited me two weeks previously. This particular reading was one I was looking forward to without knowing why.

I completed my preparations and then realized a male figure and a child were with me. I assumed they were awaiting these people. Very soon a car pulled up, and two women, one middle-aged and the other much younger, got out. As with all new clients, the usual questions were presented to me: When did you discover you could do this? How did you get into this work? Why you? After answering these questions I gave my usual talk on what to expect and what not to expect. I tried to reassure them there was nothing to be nervous about and suggested they try to stay open-minded and answer with yes or no only. I always tell people how important it is to remain open to what is being said while keeping a healthy skepticism. Problems arise when one is too close-minded. Such was the case with the clients sitting in front of me; I just did not know it yet.

I could tell by the questions the young girl was asking that she was very interested in what I did. I could sense apprehension in both of them as well as skepticism. I told them that I never made promises before a session, but today I would not only make one promise, I would make three. I promised I would not tell them that their loved ones were in a cold dark place, that I would not tell them they needed to come again for any reason, and last, that if they were not happy with their reading, there would be no charge.

We began with my asking if they had come with the hope of contacting an adult male and a child. The older woman's eyes opened wide as she turned to the younger girl, and then she looked back and said yes. I said that was good because these two had been with me for quite some time, and I wanted to make sure. I told them the male standing next to the older woman was talking about a second marriage for her. I asked if she had married for a second time. She seemed unsure of how to answer that and finally said her second husband had died. I went on to describe what I was seeing, but from that point on nothing seemed to fit. The older woman turned repeatedly toward the younger girl, who I later learned was her daughter, for clarification. The more I said, the less they seemed to understand. When something registered with the mother, in a heartbeat the daughter discredited or denied what had just been said. The daughter sat there with her arms crossed and one leg swinging over the other. I was beginning to get discouraged because I knew that the man and the child knew what they were talking about.

After about forty-five minutes, the daughter decided she had to go out for a cigarette. Perhaps I would have "better luck" if she were outside, she said. I told her what was meant to come through would, regardless of who was present, but she got up and left. Her mother said they had enjoyed the day, and if this did not work out, it was not wasted. She said, "I was afraid you would have the same accuracy with us that you had with David a couple weeks before." I asked her why she came if that was the case, and she said that although she was interested, the thought of actually communicating with those who have passed on really scared her. She didn't know how she would cope with the same successful connection I had made for her friends two weeks earlier. It became clear to me then that her fear, and the obvious fear or doubting nature of her daughter, had been able to successfully block what was being said. Her daughter returned, her arrogant energy filling the room. Now my ego was stepping in, and not only was I upset with this whole situation, but the thought of the daughter sitting there thinking I was a fraud was too much for me to handle.

The daughter began talking about how she had been to one other medium and how that situation was a total waste of time. I asked her if she had paid the medium for the session, and she replied that a girlfriend had given her the sitting as a gift. She continued telling me how she told this so-called medium she should be ashamed of herself for playing with people's emotions that way and that though she believed in the ability of mediumship, she believed 95 percent of mediums were fake.

Now I knew where I stood. She had just called me a fake; she found a way to incorporate me into the percentage she believed was taking money from unsuspecting people. At this point I checked with my guides to make sure I was still on track, even though I felt I was as far off as possible. The answer was a resounding yes.

I explained that what I was giving was the truth and that nothing else was coming through. I pulled the cassette out of the tape recorder and slid it across the table toward the mother. The daughter angrily asked, "What's that for?" I explained that it belonged to them; they should take it, and hopefully by listening to what came through later, they may realize something they had overlooked during the sitting. The daughter found it necessary to tell me this was pointless because there was absolutely nothing that related to her or her mother in any way. My hope was that if the mother listened to the tape alone, without the constant interruption and negative feedback from her daughter, perhaps something would twig her memory. I felt good when the mother slipped it into her purse and asked what she owed me. I told her she owed me nothing; this had not been a good sitting for any of us and I was certainly not charging for it. I told her at this point all we were out was a little time, and we would leave it at that. I informed the daughter that I hoped she would find the person who could help her, and I apologized for not being that person.

It was done, and I felt like I had failed miserably. Never had the spirit world let me down—what was different now? I felt good that I had not accepted money; at least if and when they talked about what transpired, the worst thing that could be said was that I was a fake. They couldn't call me a thief as well.

I have reflected on that session and asked my guides what was the purpose of it when it had left me so frustrated. The first thing I discovered was that it helped put my ego in check. It also helped me realize that I can only give out what I'm receiving from the spirit world, and that the spirit world really didn't let me down—the spirits were there and ready to communicate. Grey Owl pointed out that no matter how much a person wants to talk on a phone, it is useless unless there is someone willing to listen on the other end. Everyone who comes to me may not be ready to hear the truth. Fear grips some people so tightly that they cannot see what is right in front of them. Instead of feeling anger at them for being close-minded and/or ruled by fear, I pray they will cope with their loss and find peace. For that, I give thanks to God, Grey Owl and Gabriel. Even when I don't fully understand something, I now have faith that everything happens for a reason. Not understanding that reason does not make it wrong.

Learning the Hard Way

In my late teens and early twenties, I was a dance disc jockey. Most weekends I could be found at local dance halls spinning records. I really enjoyed my work until I discovered that I was happier enjoying the dances than being the entertainment. I loved playing the music, but I hated talking on the microphone and would tense up whenever I had to speak publicly. At the time of this incident, my days as a DJ were long over. The hall was full that night, and we were all having a good time despite the music. The most common complaint was the lack of diversity. I still had my records from when I was a disc jockey and thought I should go home and get them. Something told me, "No, don't do that," but of course because this story continues, you know I didn't listen. Not only did I bring records, but I brought a case of more than three hundred of them. I wanted to look like a big shot, the more talented disc jockey. My intent wasn't to help the disc jockey; it was to make me look good.

I marched into the hall with my case of music, walked up to the stage and set them on the table. I said, "Here you go, feel free to use any of them; please just keep them together." He looked at me and tried to smile, but he lowered his eyes and I could feel his embarrassment. I turned and walked back to my table. Elwood, a friend of my father's whom I had known since the age of five, walked up to me, poked his finger in my chest and said, "I hope you are happy with yourself—you have just humiliated that man in front of this whole audience. Who the hell do you think you are? I think you're a little asshole." He turned and walked away while I stood there dumbfounded. I really should not have been surprised; I had humiliated someone, and now the same thing was happening to me. Everyone around heard and saw what had taken place, and I was left standing with egg on my face. Aren't life's lessons grand? I tried to justify my actions by saying I wanted to help the guy out and to pass it off as Elwood's problem, but the truth is that Elwood did me a huge favour that night, and I thank him. It was painful and it was humiliating, but it was necessary. My ego required a drastic clipping of sorts, and Elwood just happened to be the one holding the shears.

We have all had experiences where we have felt stupid, didn't want to face the truth of our actions or deliberately hurt someone. My hope is that eventually we will all grow enough to be able to look back on events like this and say thank you.

No matter what your chosen career, no matter what your lifestyle or beliefs, the key to a fulfilling life starts with putting your ego in check. This is an easy thing to say but often a much harder thing to do on a daily basis because none of us wants to be wrong or embarrassed. Once you put your feelings aside and become more secure in who you really are, great things are waiting for you. To be totally free of ego is a freedom unequalled. Thinking first of the other person keeps ego at bay. Thinking of yourself first is fine as long as it is for your highest good and not for immediate self-gratification. I seem able to achieve this level in waves that have become longer with time and practice, but on occasion I still find myself knee-deep in ego. When this happens, I try to acknowledge the fact that I am not happy with the situation and that only I have the power to change it. Changing my perspective changes the outcome. Learn to laugh at yourself and try to always look at the bigger picture. By looking at a tiny object—a rock, a slice of bread or a piece of fabric—with the naked eye, you see a complete object, and your brain tells you what you are seeing. When you place that object under a microscope, a whole new world opens up to you. When you look at it from a different perspective, you can see the change, yet you are looking at the same object. It is possible for things to have two or more sides. For every perspective there is a new or different look. My gift of mediumship has broadened my beliefs, knowledge and faith, and it has changed me. I no longer say "never," because anything is possible.

Chapter 12
SCIENCE AND CHALLENGES

I have read with interest how other mediums explain the fundamentals of mediumship, but I have to be honest and say that I don't understand the exact science behind the ability of spirit communication, and I may never understand it. Others talk about vibration levels, a connection that needs to be made for successful communications, and they compare it to a telephone line. This all makes sense to me, but could I say absolutely that this is how it works? No, I could not. All I know is that it does work, and through the grace of God, I hope it continues. Helping people come to terms with death gives me an incredibly warm feeling of accomplishment. Seeing a client leave after a reading with more confidence, a new understanding of life after death and the peace that this brings tells me I helped another. For me there is no better feeling.

Chakras

We have seven main energy centres within our bodies. The Root Chakra is found at the base of the spine, and the Sacral Chakra is located a few inches higher in your lower abdomen. Next is the Solar Plex Chakra, which is located in your upper abdomen just above your waist. When you are nervous or upset and your stomach feels funny, that is your Solar Plex Chakra working. In the centre of your chest is the Heart Chakra, and in your throat area is the Throat Chakra. Moving up to the centre of your forehead, you will find the Third Eye Chakra, and at the top of your head is the Crown Chakra. Each of the seven Chakra centres or energy centres serve a different purpose, both physically and spiritually. I will not delve into them here because there are many good books already published on the Chakra System. One of the very best I have found is called, *Hands of Light, A Guide to healing through the Human Energy Field*, by Barbara Ann Brennan. It is enough to know that we have these energy centres. I will tell you that the ideal situation is to have all seven Chakras in alignment or balanced. A successful life is based on balance, whether it is spiritual, physical, work or family. Too much or too little of anything is not good.

Listen for your gut response (Solar Plex Chakra) on all issues, and you cannot go wrong. When you are not creating yourself as you want to be, stop, think and begin again. Do not criticize yourself—you cannot expect to change overnight. It took a lifetime to get where you are, and it may take the rest of your life to change. The important thing is that you are trying. The real reward is not in the destination of a trip but the journey you took to get there.

Even if the science of mediumship is not clear to me, the routines are. To ensure a clear connection is made, I take time to meditate, clear my mind and connect with the spirit world and God before every session. My exercises include opening my seven main Chakras, visualizing the specific colour that is associated to each chakra centre until a balancing occurs throughout my body. Once that is complete I check for my two friends, my guides, Grey Owl and Gabriel. Without exception, they are both there, ready to assist me. I invite all those from the spirit world who wish to come in that day and ask them to please do so in an orderly and clear fashion. I promise to give out what they give me, I promise not to hold back and I promise to do my very best for all involved. Then I say a simple prayer of thanks to God because I know even before I ask that the highest and best will be given to all involved.

Meditating is essential for me to achieve a clear and concise connection with the spirit world, and over the years I have learned how important it is for a healthy, balanced lifestyle. Anyone desiring to make contact with the spirit world should first decide why he or she wants to do this. Step two is daily meditations to achieve your desired results. If I want to get into a spiritual space and cannot meditate—for example, when I'm driving my car, I find it best not to close my eyes, and I'm pretty sure other drivers appreciate this—I have a very easy and effective way of achieving a connection to God, spirit and life. I simply play a Celine Dion CD on my car stereo. I do not know if it is because her voice is the closest thing we have to angels singing, or if the spirit world just has incredible taste when it comes to music. I do know that when her music begins, the connection to the spirit world is made instantly, and I am in a better place. Dion's beautiful voice, wonderful personality and Heaven-sent gift combine to give me a life-altering experience every time I listen to her sing. Thanks, Celine!

I know that when a connection is made to my God source, to my very essence, it is the most incredible feeling. Some of you may already know exactly what I am writing about. When I have made a successful connection to the spirit world, I am engulfed in a warm feeling usually starting at my head and flowing down the entire length of my body. This is best described as such an incredible feeling of peace that it gives me goose bumps. It can come in waves like water washing up on the shore over and over. I believe this is the most intimate experience of God's love that I am able to receive while in the physical world. I know that I am genuinely connected to God, and I give thanks for that and for all things.

Open Your Heart, and Spirit Will Come to You

The heading is taken from a Christmas song, but it is more than just a line from a song. It is a simple and beautiful way to make peace with and contact those who have passed on. When your best friend knocks on your door, you open it to greet them and welcome them into your home. The same principle applies to those in spirit; the only difference is that the door they knock on is the door to your heart. Whether you let them in or not is still up to you. The moment you open your heart, the miracles, experiences and truths are able to flow through you. This may be an emotional or mental process, but the change or shift can be felt physically. The process of opening your heart is very simple; just still your mind and your body, and then visualize yourself opening up. You may experience a pins-and-needles sensation, or it may be a wave of total calm and tranquillity that washes over you; your hair may stand on end, or it may simply be a knowing. Whatever your sign is, you will recognize it. Whether you choose to believe in life after physical death or not, your loved ones are with you, continue to love you and care for you and at times feel sadness for you. Once you choose to open yourself to them, a reunion awaits you.

Two hundred years ago, many things that were unheard of are now accepted as science. Two hundred years from now, this statement will still be true. Whether science has caught up to the "truth" or not does not make it less of a truth. A hearing-impaired person may not be able to hear sound, yet he or she can feel the music playing. The vibration of music indicates the tempo, beat and rhythm of what is being played. It is time we began to feel the vibration of life as well as listening to the sounds of it.

When I began writing this book, I believed it would be published. I have been inspired to write it. I know that what I have experienced in my life has happened for a reason, and perhaps others will gain something from my writing. I had no offers to publish; I did not even have an idea of where to begin looking for a publisher. However, I did know that it would unfold as it should. The process might take five years and fifty rewrites, but Grey Owl assured me that my future would play out as I have been shown. As a child, I felt that I was destined for greatness, that I would be happy and successful. This may sound conceited and very ego driven, but it is a statement of faith. I have come to understand that I have always been all of these things. I am what I am. What makes me great, happy or successful is my perspective of myself. It does not matter what anyone else thinks. My perspective, my truth about myself, is all that matters in my life.

If for some reason my book was not published and my gift did not become recognized on a grander scale, I would still know I have already arrived.

Greatness, happiness and success do not add up to world-renowned fame and money, just to being what you really are. The farther into this writing I got, the better I could see that this book was not as much about me as it was about life lessons, those large truths that are waiting for us to remember. We know the truths of life and the universe—we have simply forgotten them. We must learn to discover the value in all that we experience, especially those experiences that were most painful at the time.

Challenges of a Medium

We all have hurdles in life, whether we overcome them or not is up to us—our free will. How we look at these challenges will determine how successful we are in overcoming them. If we choose to avoid facing the truth, the result is usually far worse because of the stress and pressure we put on ourselves, not to mention those around you, by avoiding the issue. I can relate to this way of thinking, so I stop the cycle within myself. For me it is often self-doubt that brings hurdles to my life. It comes in many forms, and no sector of my life is immune. Knowing these hurdles are self-imposed is a big step toward accepting the situation and being able to create your chosen outcome. Accept the responsibility and stop blaming others, especially God. Know that the power rests squarely with you, and you can change. Blaming others gives your power away.

As a medium, my biggest challenge is to have enough faith in myself to deliver the messages my clients need to hear. Not all messages are what clients want to hear, but they always and unequivocally are what is needed. In order for me to do the best job I can, for those in spirit as well as those who have come to me for a session, I must repeat exactly what I am being told. Looking back on past sessions, I realize the only times I have run into trouble is when I held something back. When self-doubt creeps in and winds its roots through my mind, I hesitate and give only the information that I am confident about, often leaving out pertinent facts. Something that seems very incidental to me may be the deciding factor in my client's ability to believe this is real.

Even though I have to believe in myself and my skills as a medium, I do not rush to tell people about my ability. This could possibly be because I do not want people looking at me as though I have two heads, but I believe it has more to do with proving myself. If I am secure with whom I am and with my gift, that is all I need. I believe the changes that have occurred in my life will be evidence enough to those who know me that something fantastic has happened to me. On occasion I have felt the need to prove my ability, and this is not a good place to be. When this happens, the outcome is generally the opposite of what I was hoping for. If people choose not to believe me, that is their right. I know they will believe in life after death one day!

One other challenge I faced early on was that of fatigue. After an intense or long session, I often developed a headache in addition to being completely drained of energy. I have better control of my gift now, and I don't fight it to achieve clarity. I simply let it happen, and this has eliminated the fatigue and the headaches.

PART 2

Chapter 13
HEALING MESSAGES FROM BEYOND

Because it never occurs to me while I'm in a session that the information and details will be read by others, the way I receive and deliver messages is seldom an easily read format. I believe that very often the messages my clients receive apply to all of us, and I feel it is important that I deliver them to as many people as possible.

As a medium, I am asked many questions. One of the most frequent involves the length of time a person must be passed before they can communicate. My answer is that time seems to have no bearing on communication. The need and the genuine desire of the person seeking contact, or those from the spirit world, determine the outcome of a session. The following story demonstrates that belief beautifully.

Love Knows No Barriers

Susan is the mother of my co-worker. What made her sitting different from any other I have conducted is that Susan speaks no English. From the time her daughter booked the appointment, I felt this was going to be a healing experience for her mother. The day of the session, mother and daughter arrived on time. Because I had worked with Susan's daughter for a year and a half, I had met many of her family members who had passed on. Susan's husband had come through before, as well as her sister and a close friend.

Though I had already met these three people, the session still held many surprises for all of us that day.

What I remember most about this robust, seventy-nine-year-old lady was her constant smile. I could tell she was a warm, loving person, and as she sat there waiting for whatever was about to happen, I also knew she was a little nervous, even though her daughter had experienced spirit communication many times before and tried to reassure her mother; not knowing what to expect was hard for Susan. There was tension in the air as we began. We discussed how the translation of what I said would take place. Susan smiled and rubbed her hands in nervous anticipation.

When we began, a lady from spirit walked forward and stood next to Susan's left side. She described how cancer had stricken her in the chest area. She explained that when she was younger her hair was multi-coloured, but after her illness it went white. She described in detail how the cancer had ravaged her body, leaving her virtually skin and bones. As this woman was talking to me, I was relaying it to Susan via her daughter. I told them this lady was one generation above Susan, and I felt it was her mother. Susan was only thirty years old at the time of her mother's passing, and she confirmed that her mother had cancer and that it had left her frail. I knew I was dealing with her mother, a woman who passed away more than forty-nine years earlier.

Susan's mother told me she had three children, two girls and one boy, which Susan verified. At this point, Susan's mother bent down and kissed her daughter on the cheek. She instructed me to tell her that she was sending her a lot of love. She told Susan that she was "So happy, so very happy," and that everyone in spirit was doing fine. This beautiful lady from spirit continued telling us that Susan's determination and stubbornness had worked well in her life. She said that many people who knew Susan would not consider her a strong person, but they did not take into account the life experiences Susan had been through. What some would think of as being short-tempered or stubborn was a survival mechanism that had served her well through the years.

Then Susan's mother went on to tell me that even though it was not customary for women to work in her day, she had worked outside the home. As she was about to make way for a new person to make contact, she told Susan she had gained great strength from her while she was alive and that she loved her very much. With this information, Susan could not contain her emotions any longer, and her tears released forty-nine years of emotional pain. This would prove to be just the start of the healing that took place that day.

The next person to come through was a man who said he had been in a war. Susan confirmed that her brother had served and died in a war. He went on to say that although he'd disagreed with the war and had been afraid, he felt he had no choice, and he always tried to appear brave in front of his family and in his letters home. Susan nodded in agreement. This charming gentleman said, "You do what needs to be done, even when you know it's hard."

He went on to say he had died in an explosion. He proceeded to share with me a sense of his body falling, and I could hear explosions and gunfire all around him. Susan's daughter thought her uncle had died on a submarine and that this information was not correct, however Susan confirmed it. Susan's brother explained to them that he was taken away and he felt nothing at all from the explosion. He took this opportunity to tell Susan, "Life's blessings are really sweet and are to be appreciated."

(The next day I heard the story of Susan's brother from her daughter. Many months after his death, Susan learned from a close army friend of his that months and months of fear and turmoil had finally taken its toll, and he had deserted from the German army. His death came after he was captured and placed in a wooden box within the prison area. Susan related to her daughter how the army punished her brother for his desertion. The wooden cell that he was kept in was dynamited, and he died instantly. Susan had never talked about this before because of the sorrow that she had felt over the death of her brother, as well as the facts leading up to his death.)

After this emotional and painful trip down memory lane, Susan's husband entered in spirit and, on bended knee, rested his hands on Susan's and said, "I never left you, I never left you." Tears flowed from both mother and daughter. Erwin, Susan's husband, explained that his love for his wife had been strengthened since his death by her strength and the fact that she raised three young children on her own. Erwin passed at the age of sixty, when his youngest child was just two and half. Although twenty years separated Erwin and his wife, his death was a shock and completely unexpected. Erwin talked about the anger that Susan felt after his passing and how it had spurred Susan on to do an incredible job of raising their young family alone. He explained to Susan that when she had asked God what she had done to deserve this life, the answer was, "Great things, you have done great things; just look at your children." He went on to tell his wife and daughter that although to some greatness meant financial success and to others power, to him it meant how one acted, and she had acted with greatness.

Erwin appreciated the fact that Susan had worked two jobs at times to make ends meet; he apologized for the legal problems she was left with and for the condition his affairs were in. He acknowledged the hardships this had caused and said if the situation had been reversed, he could not have survived. He explained that as a person with little tolerance for pain, his heart attack was the perfect way out. He was also thankful that his passing was swift and, for the most part, painless. Erwin thanked Susan for raising their daughters and told her he was happy for them all, and then it was time to say good-bye.

Two days after the session, Susan's daughter told me it had done her mother a world of good. Susan had harboured a lot of resentment toward her husband for leaving her in such a financial and legal bind. Susan's finally received some much-needed closure to that part of her life, forty years later.

A Family Begins to Heal

This next family was fighting to stay intact even while trying to cope with unspeakable events. Under such circumstances, it is not uncommon for them to reach out to the spirit world for help and healing.

Two sisters and a brother came one Monday night early in January 1999 for their first session with me. The sisters, Sarah and Denise were hopeful that contact could be made with their departed family members. Their brother, Mark, confessed following the sitting that he hoped the same but believed it was all rubbish and wasn't sure what to make of this whole scenario.

Before the session began, I answered the usual questions, and after reassuring them that everything would be fine and advising them not to have expectations, we began. The first person to make her presence known was an elderly woman who took charge right from the start. If ever I thought I was in control of the session, this lady was all too willing to set me straight. She walked with confidence between Mark and Sarah. (The following account is written from memory.)

CHRIS   *This lady tells me she had a problem in the area of her breast. I am drawn to the left side. Her body shape is round on a large frame, and you need to go back two generations to your grandparents. This lady tells it as it is; she has a strong personality and says she cursed a lot. She shows me a problem with a shaking hand and arm, and she talks about two boys.*

At this point Denise spoke up and said her grandmother had three boys, but one died.

CHRIS   *Your grandmother in spirit continues to talk about the boys. She said she loved them, but they were a lot of trouble at times. She tells me her name is Evelyn.*

This bit of information surprised the three people sitting in front of me. No one was happier than me that she was able to give me her name in a way that I could understand. The level of comfort was growing in my clients, and the skepticism that Mark had shown earlier had faded somewhat.

CHRIS *Your grandmother brings love to the six of you. There must be six in your family.*

They nodded, indicating this was correct. It was now that Evelyn delivered a message to her grandson Mark, seated across from me. Her message was somewhat cryptic, but I repeated it word for word,

CHRIS *"The driest eye can shed a tear."*

He nodded his head in acknowledgement.

CHRIS *Your grandmother wants you all to know, "All will be fine; you need to stay together as a nucleus in the family."*

After delivering her messages, Evelyn pulled back somewhat to make room for another woman to step forward.

CHRIS *Another woman has come in, and this lady is telling me she had cancer in three different areas of her body. I see darker hair for this woman, and she makes references to two marriages or relationships. This lady is calling out saying, "I am fine." She is standing back and appears very hesitant. I feel this is your mother. Is that correct?*

They answered "Yes, we believe so."

CHRIS *I cannot get her name.*

Mediumship is not an exact science, and every spirit communicates differently.

MARK   *Mom's name was Rita, and she did have cancer diagnosed in three different areas of her body.*

CHRIS   *Well, your mother comes in bringing a feeling of remorse and saying she doesn't know where to start. She explains that her priorities were wrong and that she is so very sorry for this. Your mother brings you love and a gift for each of you, a gift so personal that only you will recognize it.*

Rita talked to three of her children that night. Her messages included forgiveness. She explained to her family that even if she could turn back time and change the past, she would not. Rita explained that even though a lot of it had been painful, the things they had gone through had ultimately helped shape each one of them. She told her children she should have been a kinder, gentler mother.

The family sat quietly, listening to their mother explain how her disease manifested itself because of an enduring hatred she housed in the pit of her stomach. She told them this must stop with her, that they must not carry it into the next generation. Rita talked of her first husband with a heavy heart; she did not speak kindly of him. She said he always had a need to make a fast buck. The second marriage was also connected to this man because he had remarried once again. "He is your father, and nothing can or will change this." Her words stood strong and had a visible effect on her family.

CHRIS   *Your mom is telling you something very important here, so please listen closely. "I ask that you not dwell on the negative with him; there is a good side there. It is a question of how deep you dig to see it, and it is up to you to find it, not necessarily for him to show it."*

Rita went on to discuss a third daughter not present that evening. She said this daughter lived in her own little world, sheltered as if in a cocoon or a bubble. She explained that for now this was okay, but one day she would have to look at life, and what she would see would not be pretty.

CHRIS   *Your mother tells me she had her favourites when it came to grandchildren. She is not proud of this fact; it's just the way it was.*

They smiled, laughed and nodded, confirming once again their mother was with them.

I have learned through many readings that a mother's love does not end because of physical death, and to prove it Rita told her children that she continued to help each of them heal. Whatever she was able to do to assist them, she would do. Rita talked about the time surrounding her death, and her reluctance to leave the physical world. The thought of dying had terrified her, and the reason she was terrified was because her life was not perfect. She had made mistakes and was afraid to meet her Maker. Rita reassured her children that in actual fact it was a piece of cake and nothing like she had imagined. Rita told us three people had met her at the time of her death: a young girl, an uncle who totally surprised her and a woman who had passed from a heart attack. The little girl was Rita's two-year-old niece who had passed many years before. Rita ended her meeting with her children with one more message. It was a message of hope that, if listened to, would relieve a lot of the pain of life. "Please learn from life's lessons the first time they visit you. Know that if you do not learn from the first visit, circumstances will present themselves again and again until you finally do."

The session ended after five family members from spirit had visited, but for the purpose of this book, I have concentrated on relaying only those with messages from which I felt we could all benefit.

The Follow-Up

Four months later, Sarah and Denise booked another sitting with me. After the second session, they shared some of the things referred to in their original meeting.

The sisters began to recount for me that their father had never really been there for them, and one brother was in trouble financially presently to undergo some legal problems. A third brother I had never met was in jail at that time for more than ten counts of sexual misconduct with minors and sexual assault of minors. It was through tears that Sarah told me her own son had been a victim of her brother's sickness. She still lived in the small town where these events took place.

The sadness lifted somewhat, and a spark of happiness returned when Sarah asked if I remembered telling them their mother had a gift for each of them. I did not; I rarely remembered details from any session with the exception of those that had a direct impact on me at the time. "Well, you did," she said, "and my gift was incredible and leaves no doubt that Mom's hand was hard at work." She went on to tell me that her fears were mounting as the court case came closer. Her concern was how to face the people of her hometown, a place where the ugly details of her brother's crime would be sure to come out in the local newspapers, not to mention the additional impact on her teenage son.

"Well, the ugly details never did come out in the papers—not one detail, name or reference was released to the public," she said. "I don't know how that is possible; the papers in the past have always had a field day with similar stories. All I can tell you is that Mom kept her promise and somehow saved us an incredible amount of discomfort and embarrassment. I know that was Mom's gift to me, maybe to us all, and no one can tell me differently."

Coping with unspeakable events brought about by no fault of their own, this family has endured the pain caused by one brother's actions as well as a very unsettling childhood. With love and reassurance from beyond the grave, they have been given the tools to cope and to start the healing process.

Buddy

One Thursday evening I sat waiting for the arrival of my client, Roy. Throughout the week leading up to this session, I had been feeling the presence of a male spirit whose only words to me were, "My brother, my brother," accompanied by an overwhelming feeling of anticipation. I knew that night's reading was going to be special, but I had no way of knowing the impact it would have on Roy's life—or, for that matter, on mine.

He arrived ten minutes early, and I greeted him at the door. A tall, unassuming man walked into my office, with a warm smile and very friendly energy. Before we began, I presented my usual introduction and then I told him, "I have had the impression all week that you need to speak to your brother, who is now deceased. Is that correct?"

A look of surprise crossed his face, and tears began streaming down his cheeks. His answer was very clear that the person he was hoping to make contact with would be with us. Roy wiped his eyes, and we began his reading.

Chris *I have three men standing behind you from different generations. One is standing directly next to you and seems to be indicating that he is within your generation and family. There is also a middle-aged male behind him, and an older man even further back. The man standing next to you is saying the name Thomas, over and over. Who is Thomas?*

Roy *That's one of my brothers.*

Chris *He's alive, right?*

Roy *Yes.*

Chris *Who's the "R" that is deceased, a male?*

Roy *That's my brother Ricky.*

Chris *He must have passed as a result of an accident; he is telling me it was an accident, over and over again.*

Roy   *If that's what he's saying, then I believe him, but we always felt it was deliberate.*

Chris   *He's saying, "It was an accident, Buddy, you have to believe me, and let go of your anger toward the person who did this."*

As Rick was telling his brother this, he was rubbing the back of Roy's neck with his hands in a massaging motion, calling him "Buddy" repeatedly.

Chris   *He keeps referring to you as Buddy, Roy.*

A smile spread across Roy's face.

Chris   *Now he is showing me a woman leaning down with beads in her hands, praying and crying. Is your mother a Catholic, because I am sure your brother is showing me your mother, and she is kneeling down praying holding her rosary beads. The scene seems to be taking place in her house, in a hallway.*

Roy   *All that makes perfect sense.*

Tears continued to stream down Roy's face, and I could feel him releasing his pain.

Chris   *Who is Edith, or is it Ethel?*

Roy gave a startled smile.

Roy   *"That's my mother, her name is Edith. This is unbelievable!"*

Chris   *Rick is saying, "I'm here, Buddy, you have to believe me. I am standing right next to you; I haven't gone anywhere." Now Rick gives me the name of Ashley or Ashton. It is a young girl he is talking about. Who is Ashley?*

Roy   *That is my little niece.*

Chris   *He is around her a lot, and he is talking about her eyes. Your brother is telling me that your niece has Heaven in her eyes. Please take notice the next time you see her. There is something special about her eyes. You must have a sister, Ray, because he is talking about your sister.*

Roy   *I have three sisters.*

Chris   *He is talking about a sister here, who is in a world of her own. She seems lost and always feels like a victim. This applies to only one of your sisters; the other two are completely opposite.*

Roy   *This is absolutely right, I know which sister he is referring to.*

Chris   *Your brother is showing me the date of September 13. Are you aware of the significance of that date?*

Roy sat there searching but could not think of what his brother meant by that date. I told him to remember that date because it was significant to his brother, and one day he may find out why.

Roy   *I will do my best to find out.*

Chris   *He is talking about Hollywood motion pictures; I am not sure what he is trying to tell me here.*

Roy   (smiling) *I know exactly what he is referring to.*

Chris   *The older gentleman is moving in closer to you now. He has flyaway hair that is not overly long, and a high forehead. He keeps showing me age spots all over his hands, and he is rubbing his hands. He is very self-conscious of these spots. He's also telling me he had multiple strokes and was very tired of living. He wanted to leave much earlier than he did.*

Roy   *I know exactly whom you are talking about. This man had many strokes, and you were exactly right about the age spots—he disliked them and was very self-conscious about them.*

Chris   *Now I am hearing the name George, and at the same time this man is motioning a kick in the back side to you. He is doing this repeatedly.*

Once again Roy's emotions could not be contained, and finally he said it all made sense. By now, I believed I was dealing with Roy's grandfather, so when I asked him and he said no, I was caught off-guard.

Roy   *George is the man who introduced me to Joe. It really makes sense that he would mention him.*

Rick and Joe continued talking to Roy, giving him more evidence that they were both still important parts of his life and providing much-needed proof that they were aware of what has happened in his life since they had passed on. When the session ended, Roy took the time to fill me in on a few details. The most surprising, considering the amount of emotion Roy had exhibited that evening, was that his brother Rick had passed away thirty years before.

Roy   *Rick was at a party one night and had words with another male there that he'd shared friction with in the past. That night, when Rick went to the outhouse, the other guy came out with a shotgun and pointed it at the outhouse. I guess he thought he was aiming high enough to miss him, but at the same time he pulled the trigger, my brother stood up. One single bullet hit my brother, and as he fell out the door, witnesses heard his last words, "The bastard shot me," and then he fell dead. I was fourteen years old at the time and he was twenty-one.*

*When he mentioned Hollywood movies, Rick was referring
to a painting that I have done of Bruce Lee. I am an artist
and have been trying for a long time to get my name and work
recognized. Next month a movie will be released. My painting
will be shown at the conclusion of the movie, and my name will
be included in the credits. That is what he is making reference
to—he wants me to know he is aware. The older man that
came through was Joe. I wanted to hear from two people today,
my brother and Joe, and both came through loud and clear. Joe
was my boxing coach as well as a mentor to me. Kicking me
in the backside is symbolic of how he was with me. It was great
when he mentioned George—he came to see you last fall, Chris.
He came as a total disbeliever of this kind of stuff, but he left
knowing without a doubt that his wife had come through and
was communicating with him. She said to him, "George you
have had them all, haven't you?" That statement froze him in
his tracks, because during his marriage he had been unfaithful
many times, and that was the piece of evidence that convinced
him that life goes on and that deceased loved ones really can
communicate with us. George left that day knowing you were
the real thing, and he was the one who convinced me to come
see you."*

Roy left shortly after, saying that a band of pressure was now gone from
around his head, and he felt much better. After we said our good-byes, I
could not stop thinking about this truly wonderful experience, so on Monday
morning I thought I would call Roy to see how he was doing, and ask if he
had any questions that had arisen from his session.

When I reached him and asked how he was doing, he said, "Great. I
was going to call you today. I wanted to let you know I found out the
significance of September 13. I talked to my mother and asked about that
date. She told me that Rick had a child out of wedlock that the family
was not aware of. This son passed away on September 13. It is one of

those things that my family kept quiet—no wonder he wanted me to know about that date."

Not all of my readings are this clear, and not all of them have the impact that Roy's did, but this session demonstrates how those in spirit work and how nothing stands in the way when they need to show their continuing survival and love.

Family Is Forever

As a medium, I can only give what I am being shown or told. The majority of this next session made little sense to Robin but was perfectly clear to her mother, Marge, who was also present.

I met Marge and her daughter, Robin, in 1997 at my second public talk. Following an intermission, it was time for a guided meditation and demonstration of spirit contact. As I began, I noticed a tall man standing behind a young woman in my audience, with his hands caressing the young woman's shoulders. I directed my attention to the girl, whose name was Robin.

CHRIS   *I have a male presence standing behind you rubbing your shoulders. He is a tall man with a moustache that seems larger than a typical moustache, and he appears to be in his late thirties.*

ROBIN   (Grinning) *Yes, yes. It's my father.*

CHRIS   *He tells me that he had a major impact in the chest area. I am getting incredible pressure in my chest, so however he passed, it involved his chest.*

Robin looked to the lady sitting next to her for verification. The woman said this was correct. Robin's father spent the next ten minutes talking about events in their lives and about how a change was coming for Robin. He told her how proud he was of her achievements in life.

ROBIN   *Can you see anyone else with him?*

CHRIS   *No, I cannot, I'm sorry.*

Unknown to me at that time, Robin had hoped her little brother Danny, who had also passed at the same time as her father, would come through with him that evening.

I had no other contact with Robin until almost two years later, when her mother Marge booked an appointment with me as a birthday gift for her daughter. Although I was familiar with the circumstances of the passing of both her father and her little brother, that session held surprises for all of us.

CHRIS   *A lady comes in behind you and to the right. My chest starts to fill up as she comes in, and I can now feel her presence. She is wearing a dress that is drawn in at the hips, and she is full-figured. She takes me straight to the heart area, and I get pains shooting down my arm. I attribute this to her passing. She's calling out to you, Marge. I get the letters D, E and L. She is whispering and laughing. She says orchids, orchids over and over. She is a grandmother and played the role to the hilt, she tells me. She is taking me overseas. My feeling is that she probably never was in Canada. There is a male with her who is getting a lot stronger. She's laughing again and taking me to a picturesque spot, a hill with a house built halfway up. Below the house is a small town. She tells me the beautiful picture she is showing me does not stay this way.*

ROBIN   *My mother's house is on a hill.*

CHRIS   *No, your grandmother is talking about Europe; it is overseas. There is water there as well, a river and transportation on this river. She is very clear and specific about it being a river and not a lake. She's talking about her children; she says she had three. It is important that you know she is in a white and gray chequered dress. She shows me that she has gray hair and is wearing something on her head that is not a hat. There are wisps of hair coming out at the front and sides. Her face is very weathered and textured. (I paused and interjected. _ Please don't take this the wrong way, but have you seen the* Planet of the Apes *movie? Are you familiar with the makeup on the ape's faces and how it shows the grooves and lines? This is what I mean. Believe me, I am not saying your grandmother looks like an ape. (Laughter fills the room.) She is laughing at my description of her.*

She kept tapping Robin on her right shoulder. Robin said that oddly enough she could feel it, and it was rather unsettling. Robin was not sure who this woman was, but Marge was convinced.

CHRIS   *She is not a tall woman, and she is definitely speaking a different language. Oddly enough she shows me herself outside yelling at people. She is very forceful and loud. You don't see it or feel it, Robin, but there is a real connection between you and this lady. She is constantly touching you and laughing.*

Marge interjects at this point, saying it was Robin's paternal grandmother, but Robin didn't think so.

CHRIS   *However this woman died, she laughs about it and finds it hilarious. It's like boom—she's gone. She keeps showing me facial hair, but I know it is a woman, not a man.*

This is the first time I have been shown facial hair on a lady, and by this time I had tears in my eyes from laughing so hard. Grandma was using humour to get her message across, and it was working. Robin broke out laughing, and I apologized.

CHRIS   *This woman in spirit is still laughing, she is just so happy. Your grandmother could not believe it could happen so fast. She had a good life. Other people may think the first half of her life was not that good, but she says it was. Did this woman have more than three children?*

MARGE   *She had five.*

CHRIS   *She says three again.*

MARGE   *Three are now dead, three were born in Canada, and two were born in Poland.*

CHRIS   *The three that have died, they were two males and one female?*

MARGE   *Correct.*

CHRIS   *She is telling me not to ask you any more questions; I need to focus on her more. I guess I can consider myself reprimanded. Your grandmother wants to talk about you, Robin. She says you deny yourself the sugar and sweets of life. You fall short in only one area of your life, the area where you lack discipline. She says she loves you, Robin, and she's rubbing your shoulders right now. She says, "Live grand . . . live grand." She talks about a fear of death you have. Even with all that you've experienced, you have a fear of losing those around you? She says, "Honey, it is so real when you pass over." She is now instructing me to knock on the table. "You think this table is real. What is real is the moment you pass over." She talks of the brightness of colours. Here on earth, she explains, colours are only colours, but where she is they are more—they are living, they have a vibration. You don't just see them; they have a life of their own. She is showing me a table full of food. The first thing she shows me is a long cake or pastry dessert, and I think there are apples on it.*

Robin and her mom laugh. This registered for them, and I continued.

Your grandmother tells me that fear rules half your life, and she wants to eliminate this for you. These people are having a great time over there. There is singing, dancing and celebrating going on. When something bad happens here in the physical, the party doesn't stop for them. One or two spirits leave the party for what may be fifteen minutes of our time to help or oversee, but the party continues. After visiting those in crisis, they return, knowing all will be fine. The party continues because they see the whole picture of life; they know the outcome, and the outcome is always beautiful. They need not worry for you.

Your grandmother wants you to know that you breathe life into a lot of things around you. You seem to be the focal point for a lot of people. She says that happiness is a state of mind, and she would like you to find that place a little bit more. When you are experiencing something that is not good or something you determine as negative, remember it is a state of mind. There is another way to look at it—in fact there are many ways to look at it. She doesn't want you getting stuck. Remember what you see is your perspective at that time, but it is just a matter of flipping over one or two tracks in your mind in order to see it in a different perspective. It's not an easy thing to do, but you must step aside and look at it.

Okay, now there are four more people standing between you two—two males and two females. The lady in the back is a sister to the lady standing beside you, Robin. She takes me to her neck and top of the chest area. What is really prominent here is the bone structure: her collar bone is very apparent. Marge, I need to ask you if that little description of your mother's neck area made sense.

MARGE   *Yes, it does.*

CHRIS   *She is telling me that she had a way of making little comments in the middle of conversations, flippant comments that would sting. This would hurt the other person, and she feels badly about this. She says she is so sorry and realizes now this was callous of her.*

MARGE   *This is true.*

CHRIS   *She is telling me that she hung on to physical life because she had a fear of death, and her actions while she was alive worried her. After the passing it was far better and far worse than she had imagined. The better was that she was not judged the way she thought she would be. What made it far worse was that she did the judging on herself, so she felt the emotions and the pain. Her fear was that God was going to stand there and judge her, but it never happened.*

Robin was completely surprised by this.

CHRIS   *Again she says far worse and better. There were other good things, too. She says the pain she felt during that process—I have never had someone speak about this before—was there and then it subsided. Now she can look at it and see how it helped with her growth. She says the process she talks about is like someone having a broken arm set and a cast applied: if it is not set properly, they have to go back in and reset the bone, and then the bone can begin to heal properly. This is how she is describing her life review. Once it was done, her healing could start. She would like you both to know that the one thing she had and did not know was courage. She did just fine. She says people thought she was a strong woman, but the truth was that she was strong in all the wrong areas.*

Robin's grandmother was softly stroking her granddaughter's long hair with so much kindness and love at this point.

CHRIS   *She is telling you, Robin, that nobody can cut you as deeply as you can cut yourself, so when you feel hurt, you're doing it to yourself. When someone hurts you externally, it is like a paper cut; it is minor. When it gets bigger and gets infected—this is when you know you are doing it to yourself.*

At this time, Marge's mother moved closer to her and started to laugh.

CHRIS   *She says you've been thinking of this as well, Marge. You will find this funny. She wants me to tell you she is talking about karma. She laughs because despite what people may think, it isn't true. There is no debt of any kind to repay, but she knows that you wish there was.*

Marge and her mother had a very strenuous and unhappy relationship. Years of physical abuse and alcoholism took their toll on their relationship. This detail from Marge's past had been confided in me following the reading.

She is also instructing me to tell you, Marge, that she could pick three more lives in a row, and all three could be the worst possible lives to experience, and it still would not compare to what she felt with her judgment process after she died. She wants you to know that. Now she is sitting down between the two of you, and she says she is much more relaxed. Your mother says that she could apologize, but it would do no good right now. She also says she could have come in and said all that you have experienced in your life is the sum total of who you are. She would not do that to you, and now she laughs. She puts the blame squarely on herself, and she says she was not strong enough to stop. She beat herself up over this because for all the reading, all her knowing, she could have applied it to her family life. Everything she shows me is so neat and tidy outside the house. When people looked in, they saw a perfect home, but inside was a different ball of wax. She is very serious, Marge, when she says, "So my child, today I won't say sorry, not because I don't want to, not because I don't mean it, but because today is not the day." Your mother must have had a sense of humour because she says she wants to play with you here. She tells me to use the word guide or angel here; she doesn't care which one I use. "Tell her I'm her angel," and then she laughs uncontrollably. Marge, your mom knows you don't believe this, she says it as a joke.

This woman was using humour to help heal a very deep wound.

MARGE   *I don't think so.* (She hid her discomfort with a nervous laugh.)

CHRIS   *Now the two males who are standing here want to talk. The gentleman closest to you, Robin, is your father, and even as I say he's standing, he is now sitting on a porch swing going back and forth. He is sitting there smiling, and he tells me you would sit on his lap as a young girl and swing.*

Robin shook her head no at this point, but her mother nodded yes.

CHRIS   *He is constantly giving love to all those left behind. Your father says he is so pleased and so happy for you. The spark in his eye—he is referring to you as the spark—is still there. It never went away with the accident.*

He says, "What isn't fair about death is the process that those left behind have to face. It is those who are left behind that grieve, because they do not know the beauty and peace that awaits us all." Your father wants you to know that he experiences it all; it is us who do not. He wants you to be aware of this. The loss is on our end and not his. He is explaining that he is around you all the time and is part of everything going on. He says once again that it is unfair; he says, "I am closer to each one of you now than when I was alive. What is unfair is that you don't know it and can't experience it." He says his love hasn't changed; it is just that now there is no separation. In the physical, we have distance to contend with; he does not. He is telling me his uncle met him at the time of his passing. After the accident he may have lived, but he tells me he was gone even before the impact. He was removed from it; he did not have the physical pain to contend with. He explains that he was disoriented at first and a little angry because he didn't understand what was going on. He was not comfortable with that feeling.

Now your brother Danny is here, Robin. He has put flowers on your lap for your birthday. He shows me pink flowers coming out from one side of the bouquet. He has a sense of humour and laughs, saying he was a chicken, a coward, and he got out early. You have to stay and play, but he got out early and he says you can have it. (He refers to physical life). Danny says his luck is your loss because Dad came with him. That was important to him. He certainly doesn't say this to be mean. This is how he sees it. Life's lessons are so hard, he says. It is so permanent and one-sided when a person suffers the loss of a loved one. In a perfect world, it would not be that hard on people. He is not comfortable with the hurt and pain that we feel at the loss of our loved ones. Those who experience what we call death don't feel the pain because they are not ripped apart like those of us left behind.

Marge and Robin agreed. The energies began to withdraw after approximately two hours. A feeling of accomplishment fell over me, and my world was good. I was truly blessed to be able to relay life-changing messages to the living from those loving spirits who resided beyond the veil.

Chapter 14
WHEN OUR CHILDREN LEAVE US

We all know people who seem to have had more than their share of life's tragedies, and we often wonder how they cope and manage to move on. I believe moving forward after a tragedy or setback in life is a personal and conscious decision. I also believe those with some of the greatest hurdles in life are parents who have lost a child. No greater loss can be experienced by a soul. To have such a vital part of your life now gone leaves a wound so deep, so personal that it never truly heals.

My life as a medium has provided me with many opportunities to sit with families that have lost children. It is an honour for me to convey the messages of these children to their parents and siblings. It is for all the families I have sat with, and those I will sit with in the future, that I tell the following stories. These are true accounts that I believe show our children never truly leave us. In some way, they have always been a part of us and always will remain so. Those who have passed over transcend space and time to remain an integral part of their family. I have chosen stories that show love never dies and that even from beyond the grave. our children talk to us. The question is, are we listening?

Ryan's Story

While driving to Toronto, I knew there was something special in the air, though exactly what that was, I would not discover until later that evening.

I finished preparing for my seminar at the Holiday Inn downtown when a young couple entered. They were both wearing nervous smiles as they took their seats. I greeted them and sensed an overwhelming sadness unlike any I had experienced before.

When this couple came in, I glimpsed a little boy from spirit, walking in with them. As soon as I saw him, he disappeared. When I started the evening off, this couple continued to captivate my attention, and I knew something special was about to happen.

Paul and Rose Hill were a young married couple who were living every couple's dream in a rural setting, until one morning in July 2001.

The following account is transcribed from Paul and Rose Hill's cassette tape from that evening.

CHRIS   *It's a male presence that I am getting with a D and N connection, like Darren or Don. Is there a reason why there is a younger male standing in front of you? I don't know his connection to you yet, but he has been chomping at the bit since the beginning of the night. Something unexpected or sudden happens, but there is a window of opportunity where people get to talk to him. I don't know if people think he is not aware of it or not, but he is and he wants you to know that he hears you, and then he passes. This is a very calm time when people talk to him, but there is a clinical or health-related situation that he is referring to.*

PAUL   *Yes.*

CHRIS   *Was he that young, or is there a reason why I am getting a four?*

ROSE   (crying) *No.*

CHRIS   *Just remember I said that. He is acknowledging something about four.*

ROSE   *Okay.*

CHRIS   *He is there with an older male. I think the male is connected to Paul. He wants you to know he's there, and it comes through as Grandpa, but he is there with the older male, and he wants you to know that he is taken care of.*

(Paul starts to cry harder and nods yes.)

CHRIS   *He is punching you in the arm (indicating this to Paul), and he keeps doing these little jabs in the arm to you. He has been giving you signs at home, left, right and centre; be open to them. Some you get and some you don't, he says. Watch for all the signs; it's as if you are closed off at home. Someone is referring to having a lingering disease or health ailment before passing. There is something very drawn out about someone's passing. It feels that he is referring to someone older.*

ROSE   *Okay, okay.*

CHRIS   *Somebody ... there is a filling up of fluids in the lungs and heart area. He wants you to know he is okay. He just wants to promise you he is okay and that he loves you.*

(Rose and Paul both cry and acknowledge what has been said.)

CHRIS   *He says you are silly (pointing to Rose). What are you silly about? He says you're silly.*

(Rose drops her head and weeps.)

CHRIS   *Was the D and N his name? Where does the D and N come in? They are acknowledging this again.*

ROSE   *I don't know.*

PAUL   *Could be Uncle Donny.*

CHRIS   *He just gave me a G. He is telling me that somebody had to make a decision about turning something off, and it's okay. It's okay. Somebody had to turn something off and make a decision to end it. It's okay.*

(Rose and Paul are both very emotional at this point.)

CHRIS   *Is this your son? He says, "It's okay, it's okay, I just want you to know it is okay, that you made the right decision ... You had to make that decision. Do you know how many people would not have been strong enough to make that decision? Strong enough, brave enough and unselfish enough to do that." A lot of people would have lingered and lingered, hoping, and he says there was no hope. You made the right choice; he had to go ... he had to go. and whoever decided ... it was fine. Just so you are aware, he showed me an air-compressor tube thing stopping, that somebody had to hit a switch.*

ROSE   *Okay.*

CHRIS   *He says, "You are the best, the best." Does he have a younger sister?*

ROSE   (crying harder now) *Yes, yes!*

CHRIS   *He is acknowledging the younger sister and for you to throw all your energy into her and not him. He's fine, he's around you. Throw your energy into the younger sister. He says she's cute. He probably wouldn't have said that when he was here.*

(Rose laughs out loud upon hearing this.)

CHRIS   *He is acknowledging her being cute and really needing your time and energy. Was there a conversation on your way here over music stations on the radio or something? He's making me feel like he sat in the backseat and listened to you have this conversation over the radio stations.*

(Rose laughs again.)

CHRIS   *He says Grandma is going to be okay. I believe he talking about your mom (pointing to Rose). So there is something about Grandma being okay.*

ROSE   *Yep, yep ... okay.*

CHRIS   *There is a health issue that people are already aware of, and he says she will be okay. He is showing some kind of sports thing, and I don't know what this is exactly. It's connecting to you, there is some pride issue (pointing to Paul), but it's a sports feeling tagged to it. It almost feels like it would be displayed or framed or ...*

PAUL   *I know what it is.*

CHRIS   *It's sports related, it's framed or mounted up on something, it's something for people to see, and there is glass, I am seeing the glass.*

PAUL   (to Rose) *It's your hockey helmet on him.*

CHRIS   *But, he is connecting to you* (pointing once again to Paul). *Is there glass in front of it, either framed or—*

PAUL   *Yes ...*

CHRIS   *Is your dad's death really sudden? Because—*

PAUL   *Yes.*

CHRIS   *There is a very sudden, very fast feeling, an unexpectedness coming up around this. Who is the M name? There is an M name.*

PAUL   *Our daughter ...* (crying)

CHRIS   *Oh, Grandpa's taking care of her. I thought Grandpa was taking care of your son. He says that Grandpa is taking care of—and he gives me the M. I thought his name would have been Mikey or Mark or something because of the M. Grandpa is watching over the little sister a lot ... a lot. There is something about music, and you in a car singing ... I don't know what I am hearing, like older music ... it's like I am supposed to tease you.*

ROSE   *Oh God!* (laughs)

PAUL   *That's what it is.* (laughs)

CHRIS   *He's got me in the car, though.*

ROSE   (both laugh) *Yeah, yep.*

CHRIS   *You're not making this fit though, right!*

PAUL   *Oh no, no ... no. I know exactly what it is.*

CHRIS   *He mentions a picture and says that time moves on. There is a real need for you to continue on with life and know that he will be with you. There is a feeling that you have somehow have tried to stop time, or you keep it closer to the time he was here. Does that make sense to you? He wants you to march forward, knowing that his photos, his stuff will come with you no matter where you are going, no matter what life brings you. He is there with you, almost as if in a physical sense. He's there in his energy, in his soul; you can't stop time.*

        Do you have a "no no" room? My aunt had a "no no" room, where things were kept that you are not allowed to touch. Is there something done for him that you don't want people doing?

ROSE   *No.*

CHRIS   *He is making reference to my great aunt's room. We were never allowed in there. You could stand at the door and look at all her dolls, but you could not go in because you were a kid. He makes me feel that there is a room in the house you tried to keep for him, and there is a time-related thing for him. He is showing me—is it just over the two ... two something. He's showing me the number two, and it is time-related. I don't know if it's months or years, but he is showing me it's just over the two.*

PAUL   (crying) *Yeah! It was his age.*

CHRIS   *Two! Oh, he's a little gaffer. I kept seeing four earlier and I thought four years old. Now he's showed me the two.*

PAUL   *Keep going, I will tell you the story after.*

CHRIS   *There is something about a dog; he's acknowledging something about a dog.*

PAUL   *There?*

CHRIS   *I don't know, is it a beige, brown colour? I'm seeing the colour of a golden retriever, but it's not a retriever. He is acknowledging something to do with the neighbours as well ... something about dogs external to you. You honestly thought your heart had broken, but he says you know it hasn't because you've gone on, and that is a great thing. He shows me the funeral part, and he says that's where you thought there would be no tomorrow. He says you know there have been many tomorrows; life goes on and he's with you, he wants you to know. He's two years old and can communicate this well! I have had sixty-year-olds that can't communicate this well.*

ROSE   (laughs) *He's pretty special.*

CHRIS   *His sister is fine, he wants you to know she is fine. Whatever has happened to him, she is bypassing it; she's on a different road than he was.*

PAUL   *Whew!*

CHRIS   *Were there spells or something before his passing? He shows me his eyes rolling back in his head. I don't know what this represents. I don't feel like this is his actual passing. There is something before that he wants to address about his eyes rolling back. It feels like a little spell or something he took. I don't know why, but he is addressing that.*

PAUL   *Anything to do with Hydro?*

CHRIS   *I don't know, he is just showing me his eyes rolling back into his head, and it's like a spell, before he dies ... that's all he is showing me.*

PAUL   *Yeah, yeah ...*

CHRIS   *He says he has to go now, but he's still with you. He is standing behind you, and you know he's here. He wants you to know you had much more with him than many get in a lifetime because they can't have kids. It doesn't bring you comfort, I know, but he wants you to know whatever the two-year window was ... was more than a lot of people get.*

CHRIS   *What was his name?*

Both Paul and Rose spoke in unison: Ryan.

CHRIS   *I am so glad he spoke up. I knew from the moment you walked in that there was something ... and I didn't know what. I thought, My God, they drove from Stratford! Before I started, I was up there with my back to you, and I said, "Whoever is here for them, please let them come through." I know no matter what happens now, I will drive home tonight being okay!*

PAUL   *You were right on with everything.*

CHRIS   *I'm glad if it brings you comfort and that you know he is here ... that's all I care about. It's not about me being right or wrong.*

I moved on at this point to the rest of the people in attendance that night, although Ryan was not quite done yet. Over the course of the next forty minutes, unbeknownst to me, Ryan came through several more times, giving me the name Thomas, which nobody claimed. He also gave me a "Z" name, which I could not hear properly, and again nobody claimed.

Following the seminar, Paul and Rose walked up to thank me and to let me in on a few more details about Ryan. Paul reached into his front pocket and said, "Do you remember the Thomas nobody claimed? That was Ryan, I am sure of it." As his hand came out of his pocket, I could see a small wooden toy. Opening his hand I saw the smiling face of Thomas the Tank Engine. "This was his favourite toy," exclaimed Paul, wearing the biggest smile I had ever seen. I was shocked.

Then Rosie came forward and said, "Remember the Z?". I just looked in amazement as she pulled out a single wooden puzzle piece of a Zebra. "These were the only two items of his we brought. I know he was letting us know that he knew."

"Why didn't you speak up when those names and references came through?" I asked.

Paul looked at me with eyes filled with sorrow and relief and said, "You spent so much time with us; we didn't want to monopolize the time for others here." Even after suffering the most horrendous loss, the Hills still were considerate of others. What wonderful people they are. Needless to say, the Hills hold a special place in my heart, and Ryan's story continues to have a life-changing effect on me. I thank them for letting me include their story. It is my hope it will help others come to terms with life's most difficult experience, the loss of a child.

I invited the Hills to share their personal story in their own words. The following account was provided by Paul Hill.

> We found out that Rosie was pregnant in the fall of 1998. Rosie was ill every day, and her sickness never subsided, even on the way to the hospital. Rosie did everything by the books while she was pregnant: she didn't smoke or drink, and she even gave up caffeine, including Coca-Cola, her favourite drink. On Saturday, August 14 at 1:32 p.m., after a short labour of only two and a half hours, Ryan Paul William was brought into our lives.

We had worried about how our Rottweiler, Sam, would accept him, but they got along remarkably well. Ryan and Sam quickly became inseparable friends. Right from the beginning, we knew that Ryan was above average; he was extremely alert to all of his surroundings.

Not long after we brought Ryan home, we discovered that he was colicky. We would walk with him in our arms all night and then work in the barn all day. We jokingly threatened him that we were about to put him in a beer case and send him to Toronto to live with the homeless. It was during this time that Ryan earned the nickname Boo-Man, because he seemed to be crying (boo-hooing) all of the time.

Ryan remained colicky for about six months. We tried every supposed cure in an attempt to treat Ryan's colic, including listening to classical music, of which neither of us was very fond. Unfortunately for us, Mozart was the only person who could calm our son.

One night, Ryan slept through the entire night. We immediately thought that something must be wrong, but he was just being an unpredictable new child. He was beautiful, and he was perfect. We did everything together as a family, and at only three months of age we started Ryan on swimming lessons. The three of us went to dinners, weddings and parties—we did everything with him. Ryan had a charisma about him, and everyone that we met commented on how beautiful he was, whether it be his golden blonde hair or his big blue eyes. Ryan loved riding in combines, tractors or any kind of trucks; he loved being with his parents.

We lived on a farm, so Ryan's first words weren't words at all, but animal noises. These noises later developed into small phrases: "No way," "Right there," and "What's that?"

Ryan was never sick; he was as healthy as a horse. Rose and I went on a cruise, our first vacation in five years, and we left Ryan with my sister Judy and her family. She promptly introduced him to ketchup and hockey. Ryan loved hockey, and he would run with his mini hockey stick and hit a ball for hours. One of our favourite pictures of Ryan hangs on our wall, with him putting on his mommy's hockey helmet. It depicts a sense of pride that only a parent could feel.

In June, my mother, who watched Ryan every day while we were in the barn, noticed Ryan's stomach getting a little bigger. He also wasn't able to hold a lot of food down without bringing it back up. We took him to our family doctor, where blood was taken, and we were told that his liver wasn't functioning normally. At twenty-two months of age, Ryan was about to be introduced to his first hospital visit. On July 1, 2001, the Canada Day long weekend, we went to a hospital in London for sick kids. It was a hospital renowned for it specialty in certain fields, one of which was cancer treatment. It was also a hospital that we had driven by a hundred times before, on our way to a mall or while going out to dinner with friends, and we had never given it a second thought. As a matter of fact, we even had trouble finding the right entrance. It was a place with which we were about to become all too familiar. Later people would tell us that we were lucky to live so close to such a hospital, but if we were really lucky, we wouldn't be at the hospital at all!

We had two cousins that worked as pediatricians at that hospital. Gary and Jane were off that day but promised us that we'd have answers by the end of the day. They took blood tests and did ultrasounds (which I always thought were just for pregnant women) and CT scans. Halfway through the day, Gary told us that he suspected cancer. To us, this was the worst thing he could have said. My first instinct was, No way, this can't be happening. When we asked how serious this was, Jane appeared at the door behind Gary. Knowing she'd come in on her day off was when we realized how serious this was. By the end of the day, I had learned more terminology than I cared to recall.

"Oncology" was a word I didn't know when I came in, but I can't seem to forget it now. Our world was starting to crumble—how could this be happening to us? We were just regular people who lived on a farm, outside of a small town.

That Friday night, July 1, Rosie and Ryan spent the night at the hospital so that the doctors could do more tests Saturday morning. Rosie told me the next day that during the night Ryan woke up and looked at her and said "No way," like he knew something horrible was going on but couldn't believe it was happening. These were the last words that Ryan ever said at the hospital. We made a pact: Ryan would never be by himself at the hospital, and we honoured it for two and a half months.

There are two types of liver cancer, hepatoblastoma and hepatocellular carcinoma. The test results, after performing a biopsy on the tumour in our son's stomach, kept coming back inconclusive. Samples of the tumour were sent to Toronto and Texas. Hepatoblastoma is the most common form of liver cancer in children. Even being the most common, it only occurs in one in five million children.

On Thursday, July 19, during the night, Ryan's stomach increased five centimetres in diameter. Ryan's tumour was growing at a horrific rate, so the following day, the hospital moved him to PCCU (the pediatric critical care unit). It was here that we had to decide whether to start chemotherapy. Without it Ryan was going to die, but the chemotherapy might kill him as well. We were told the side affects of the chemo, some of which were heart problems, hearing loss, and vision problems, along with the commonly known hair and weight loss. It was also here that we learned about hepatocellular carcinoma, the second form of liver cancer—the form that is incurable. We were told that there was little chance of this type of cancer occurring in Ryan because of his age. Hepatocellular carcinoma tended to only strike kids three years old and older. Ryan was flying under the radar at twenty-three months. So without any definite test results, and a tumour growing at an alarming rate and shutting down organs and killing Ryan, we decided to try the chemo. If nothing happened, we wouldn't put Ryan through any more treatment and would let our son go with dignity.

Chemo began on Saturday, July 21, and on Monday at noon, Ryan stopped breathing. His eyes rolled back in his head, and he had to be put on a ventilator because he could no longer breathe on his own. He was moved to a private PCCU room in a coma, and that night the doctors asked us what our wishes were, when (not if) his heart stopped. We decided not to have it restarted. We called our family and friends, and we waited together all night. We were so lucky to have the friends and family that we have. During that night, Rosie and I both told Ryan that if he had to go, it was okay, and we wouldn't be angry with him. We told him how much we loved him, and we told him how proud we were of him. At about 3:00 a.m., to the surprise of everyone, his vital signs turned around.

For the next week Ryan remained unconscious in PCCU, with more tubes sticking out of him than you can imagine. Never once was he left alone. Friends and family came when Rosie and I could no longer stay awake, and they read to him 24/7, always letting him know that someone was there. On Monday, July 30, Ryan woke up and was taken off the ventilator. I arrived at the hospital, and for the first time in almost a week, Ryan looked at me with his arms outstretched for a big hug.

Ryan's stomach was larger than that of a woman who was nine months pregnant. The skin was pulled so tight that it could not be pinched, and every vein was clearly visible. It looked as if it would tear or burst at any second.

Every day I played with Ryan's stomach to see if the tumour had subsided. On Friday, July 27, I thought I noticed his skin had a little play. The chemo seemed to be working. On August 8, Ryan had another CT scan, and it showed that the tumour had shrunk 15 percent from the *original* CT scan. All that the doctors had wished for was to stop the growth of the tumour.

The times that we wished our child was going to be the miracle child and walk out of the hospital seemed to be happening. Everyone was so excited, and we couldn't believe it.

The next round of chemo was to start on August 13, so we were allowed to bring Ryan home on the weekend for days only, and boy did he love it. After round two of chemotherapy was over, we were allowed to bring Ryan home again, this time to spend nights with us (as long as we had home care come in) for almost two weeks. Ryan came home on August 23, and every night when we went to bed, I'd carry Ryan up the stairs, and he'd give me the biggest hug a dad could ever hope for. During this time at home, something strange happened at nights: at 3:00 a.m. Ryan would wake up and point and wave at something on the ceiling.

We didn't notice any change at all after the second round of chemo, and on September 1, our worst nightmare came true. When I was bathing Ryan, I noticed three new lumps on his lower abdomen. We knew it could only mean one thing: the chemo had killed the hepatoblastoma cells, but the hepatocellular carcinoma cells were ravaging his body and creating new tumours.

Ryan went back to the hospital on September 4 for another CT scan, and we received the results the next day. Ryan had pretty much told us the results without the doctor's saying a word, when he pointed at the door and yelled, "Home! Home! Home!" (words he had never said before), meaning to take him home. It was Wednesday, September 5, when we decided to take Ryan home and "love him to death." What a decision that was for us to make—to take him from the hospital where everything gets fixed, and people go home happy to continue their lives and to pick up where they'd left off. However, when you have three oncologists giving you their blessing, and your two-year-old son pointing at the door, you just hope you are making the right decision. How unfair it would have been to have Ryan pass in a place that he had hated so much. We took him home and surrounded him with the things he loved: Mommy, Daddy, his dog, his cat, his toys and his books.

When Ryan was home, he was still waking up every night at 3:00 a.m., pointing and waving at the ceiling as if to say hello. He did this every night until he passed. At the time we didn't understand this.

As a parent, it saddened me that I would never hear my son say he loved me, something that so many people take for granted. On Monday, September 10, at 3:00 in the morning, as Ryan and I looked at each other, he spoke his last words: "I love you, Dad." This was such bitter irony. I had wanted to hear it so badly, but I also now realized that it was the last thing my son was ever going to say to me, and his time with us was getting very short.

On Tuesday, September 11, 2001, Ryan was failing quickly, and family and friends surrounded us. Ryan held on until Wednesday, September 12, at 1:32 a.m., and he passed, lying in his most favourite spot in the world: in bed with his mommy and daddy beside him. This was his safe spot, and he knew he was safe lying between Mom and Dad; he could always reach over and touch either one of us. We said our good-byes, and then we called the doctor and the undertaker, changed his diaper and put on his favourite pajamas. I walked my son around the pool, telling him how proud I was of him and how much we loved him.

The doctor came and pronounced Ryan dead, and the undertaker came and placed Ryan in the hearse. At exactly 3:00 a.m. on September 12, Ryan's body left home, but not his spirit. That morning I lowered our flag to half-mast, and we started calling friends and family. Ryan's little tummy was as large as it had been in the hospital. The undertaker told us it was filled with cancerous fluids. We thought our hearts were broken forever, but never once did we feel that Ryan was in the casket. When we got home at night, we could always feel his energy.

Three weeks after Ryan died, we went up the stairs as usual to go to bed. It was a warm fall night, but as soon as we got to the top of the stairs, it turned freezing cold, and we knew we were going to have a visitor. At about 1:30 a.m. there was an overwhelming smell of the baby cream that we used on Ryan. The smell lasted for about five minutes, and we both knew that the only jar that we had of that cream was downstairs in a closed bathroom cupboard. Rosie knew it was Ryan's way of telling her he was there. The same night at about 3:00 a.m., I woke up and I heard Ryan's voice, telling me that he loved me again. This was our first definite experience with Ryan's spirit.

Time moved on, and we were blessed with a beautiful baby girl on December 12, 2001, three months to the day that Ryan died. We named her Madeline Rose, and she is truly a gift. During our grieving process, we started watching John Edward on television. John Edward is a spiritual medium who connects with the dead and conveys messages to their families and friends. Seeing this, Rosie started looking for a spiritual medium to book a reading. Chris, not unlike John Edward, did readings and was conveniently just an hour and a half away. Rose asked if I would like to go to his seminar and see if we could contact with Ryan, and I jumped at the chance.

I told my mother about Chris and what we were planning. Being the skeptic that she was, she asked us why. I told her that it might answer some questions that we had, like whether we had made the right decision in discontinuing the chemo, cutting Ryan's short life even shorter. I also wanted to know whether or not Ryan was with my father, who had passed in 1973 after driving into a tree while having a heart attack. We also wondered if Maddie was going to be okay and hoped the cancer was not genetic. Last, I wondered if our old Rottweiler, Sam, who had passed the year before, was there to protect Ryan.

The day came when we were to go see Chris. We told Ryan we were going and asked him to be with us if he could. With pictures in hand, a small tape recorder, Ryan's favourite toy (Thomas the Tank Engine) and a toy zebra, an animal that Ryan would often imitate, we set out. On the way to Toronto, we discussed the weather, the news and the music selection on the radio.

When we got to Toronto and entered the building, we saw Chris at the front of the room. He looked up and stared right at us. Later he told us he knew we were going to be "the ones" that night. The readings began, and Chris came to us right away. One of the first things he said was that there was a little boy standing between us. We both knew immediately it was Ryan—he was coming through!

We taped the session so we could listen to it in detail later. I will quickly summarize what was said. Ryan was with my father; the reference to the "older male" verified this. Maddie was going to be okay. To find out that Ryan knew that he has a little sister, and that he knew her name began with an "M," is amazing. Sam was protecting our son, just the way she used to when we brought Ryan home from the hospital as a baby. The question that we wanted, *needed* answered so badly was whether we had made the right decision about stopping the chemotherapy—and we did. Ryan assured us that it was okay. That was all we needed to know.

There were many other validations as well, such as Ryan teasing his Mommy about being "silly," which is something she always accused him of being; and teasing us about what Ryan called "old music," which of course was his beloved Mozart. Ryan mentioned he was riding in the backseat that night and recalled some of our conversation as well. Near the end of the tape, a "T" for "Thomas" came up that was never claimed during the reading. We were sure it was in reference to the Thomas the Tank Engine that I had in my pocket. At the end of the session, a "Z" name was mentioned, and no one claimed it; we were sure that was for the zebra we brought along as well. Ryan hadn't left and wasn't finished with us.

What an incredible experience it was to have so much accurate information given to us, to have our four questions answered and our minds opened to one more aspect of our beautiful, brave son. He is still with us, only in a different way than we are used to. Many people have asked us if the reading gave us a sense of closure, and we always reply, "Not closure but comfort."

We honestly believe that Chris is genuine, and we believe that there is more to death than anyone realizes. We would like to take this opportunity to thank Chris again for all his help with the readings. We will go back sometime soon, to connect with Ryan again.

Number One Mom

How does a single mother with three children cope with the fact that her son has but a few short weeks left of life? This is a question I had as I thought about Kim Major. Kim came into my life after I accepted an invitation by her mother, Ruth, to come to her home one evening last year to demonstrate my ability for her family and friends. This would be my second meeting with Ruth. During my first reading with Ruth, I discovered she had lost her daughter Corrie as a result of a vehicle accident and that another family member was suffering from cystic fibrosis.

That evening at Ruth's house Corrie alluded once again to the person with the breathing issue and how it was progressively getting worse. I was later told that Corrie was talking about her sister Kim's son, Justin. I could feel the pain Kim was experiencing at being a helpless bystander, unable to solve her son's problem.

Months passed from that October night, and in March, the following year, Kim called to book an appointment. The sadness I often hear on the phone from grieving souls is not new to me, but the grief still can take me by surprise. Kim told me that Justin had passed and that she needed to make a connection with him; she felt ready. She wanted her reading as soon as possible. I flipped through my calendar, but the earliest I could see her was two months away, on May 9, 2002, just three days before Mother's Day. I later found out Justin had a reason for the timing. Two months was far too long for a grieving parent to wait, but Kim agreed and was very understanding. On May 7, just two days before we were to meet, I called to confirm the appointment. As I was hanging up the phone, there stood Corrie and Justin in my family room. Justin stepped forward and asked if I would buy his mother a Mother's Day gift for him because this was her first Mother's Day without him. I had never been requested to do anything like this by someone in spirit, and even though I said yes immediately, I had no idea how to handle this. Silly me, I didn't have to worry about anything; Justin would handle all the details.

It was the day of Kim's reading and I still had not gone shopping for a gift. I didn't know where to begin. The day before I was out and was asked by Justin to shop, and in all honesty I ignored his request, hoping that I would not have to go through with this awkward chore. No such luck—he expected me to do this for him and had no problem stating plainly that I had promised.

I went to the first store and immediately found the perfect card. It talked about the perfect mother who had experienced more in this lifetime than many mothers have to. I bought it immediately, but the perfect gift eluded me. Nothing felt right. As I left that store, I told Justin that if he wanted me to do this, he had to help me out. Then the idea came to me to go to a jewellery store in another town, ten minutes away. One hour before Kim's appointment, I walked into the jewellers and asked the two salespeople if they had any Mothers' Day pendants available. They walked me to the front of the store and opened the jewellery case to a whole panel of Mother's Day charms. Great, I thought, which one? Each saleslady had her personal choice, and I wasn't sure. Suddenly Justin stepped up and said, "Please buy the one on the left." I looked at the saleslady and made the choice: a small gold heart with the words "#1 Mom" written across it. It was perfect.

Following an emotion-packed session with Kim and her mother, Ruth, I told Kim of Justin's request and watched as the tears welled up in her eyes. I handed her the tiny gift-wrapped package and card. She sobbed tears of anguish and said she just couldn't open this now and hoped I understood.

I informed Kim I did not care if she ever opened it; I was simply asked by Justin to do this for her. I had done what he asked, and honestly that was all I was concerned about.

Then Kim told me how much she was missing Justin and how the Valentine's Day that had just passed since his death had been exceptionally hard. "Justin was always the thoughtful one," she said. "He would make or buy something for me on special occasions. Last year on Valentine's Day, Justin made me a special card and artwork and left it on my bed, so I would see it when I arrived home. I still have it hanging up on my mirror. I love looking at his hand drawn heart and the '#1 Mom' he wrote on it for me. I will always cherish it."

A lump formed in my throat. I said, "Well, you will love what he got you today," and I grinned. A warm sensation flowed down through me, and I knew that Justin had hit another home run.

About two weeks later, I heard from one of the salesladies in the jewellery store that the owners of the store were casual acquaintances of Kim's family. The story just blew everyone away. What a small world, I thought, especially considering Kim's family lived an hour away.

I have talked to Kim since that night, and she still cries when she thinks about the pendant and card. "But," she says, "I know that Justin is still with me."

Joni's Good-bye

Mamma you gave life to me
Turned a baby into a lady
And mamma all you had to offer
Was a promise of a lifetime of love

The above lyrics are from a Celine Dion song called "Good-bye's (the Saddest Word)." The lyrics are haunting and poignant and describe the heartbreak of having to say good-bye. People are different, unique individuals; we vary in our tastes, likes, dislikes and even on social issues of what is acceptable and what is not. Losing a loved one, and especially a child, is a hurt unlike any other, and parents all grieve differently. Some parents find strength and clarity following the death of a child, and they are able to move on and function, but others seem to be stuck in the grief. Those stuck in the grief actually die a little each day after the loss of a child. I can't pretend that I know how these parents feel, but what I do know is that moving ahead in life is a choice and one that only the individual can make.

Often I hear in sessions those in spirit ask their surviving loved ones how long they would be in the company of a chronically depressed person? Regardless of how much you loved the person, how long do you think you could do it before it affected your health and mental state?

It truly is no different for those in spirit. If you are constantly depressed, sad and in an all-encompassing darkness, why would anyone choose to be with you for long? Our loved ones try to help us, but we have to take the first step and help ourselves. This next story is about a woman whom my heart goes out to, and her beautiful sixteen-year-old daughter Joni.

I received a call for an appointment from a woman who said her name was Dianne. She'd gotten my name from a friend, and as we talked, I realized I was becoming progressively sadder. The heartbreak I felt over the phone was crippling, and before I could provide Dianne with possible dates for her reading, she did what no client should ever do: she was so desperate to heal and to make contact with someone that she said she lost her daughter and needed to see me as soon as possible.

I was taken back by her forthright approach, because I am used to people giving only that information or showing only those emotions they want to share. In all honesty that is the way it should be. I asked Dianne to please not provide any additional information and that I would see what I could do to get her in as soon as possible.

The day of Dianne's appointment, I waited patiently for her to arrive. The minutes ticked by and Dianne did not arrive. While sitting in my office and getting somewhat aggravated, a wonderful energy swept over me, and I heard the words, "Please don't be angry with my mother; she is coming." Instantly my feelings changed from anger to peace and tranquility.

Within a few minutes I saw this tired, rundown, gentle soul walking toward me, asking if I was Chris. "Yes, nice to meet you, Dianne," I said. I explained to her that although she had told me who she was needing to hear from, I could not guarantee that I would be successful in making contact. She nodded, but I know she didn't or wouldn't accept that as a possibility.

From the very start Joni was present, conveying her feelings, thoughts and impressions vividly, clearly and with great purpose. Although I was aware that Dianne had lost her daughter, that was the full extent of what I knew.

Joni talked about being outside when she passed. She impressed on me that she was pushed from behind and that she was not alone at the time. Her mother confirmed she was outside and could validate the push from behind, but she said she could not validate that she was not alone. Joni repeated that she was not alone and that she had died due to head trauma. Dianne did not understand the statement of her being with someone. I felt that she had been hit by a car or pushed from behind while outside. Joni talked of her sisters, her little step-brother and her baby nephew, whom she adored. She talked about her mother's grief and the steps she would have to take to find healing. Tears and pain exuded from Dianne throughout the course of the reading. It wasn't until the end of the reading that her mother filled me in on her complete story. Dianne explained that sixteen-year-old Joni had gone to her grandparents house in another city for the weekend. While there, Joni went outside with her headphones on for a walk. Without a care in the world, this vibrant teenager walked and sang her favourite songs, unaware of the danger that was fast approaching her from behind.

Never in her wildest dreams did she think she was in danger, and yet in a heartbeat the lives of her family and all those who knew her would be changed forever. Speeding behind her and without any possibility of stopping was a locomotive train bearing down. Although Joni was not on the tracks, she was walking on the side and close enough so that when the train passed her, the hand rail that sticks out from the engine impacted Joni's head from behind, pushing her forward to the ground. She was killed instantly.

Although Dianne was very pleased with her reading and believed beyond a shadow of a doubt that Joni had in fact survived her tragic death and was sitting next to her communicating through me, this still did not take away the pain of her loss. I spent a great deal of time with Dianne that day. Not knowing why, I felt I had a special bond with her.

Two months later Dianne came back for a second reading and brought her oldest daughter, who was having an extremely difficult time adjusting to the loss of her sister. Once again Joni did not disappoint her family. What struck me about Joni was her ability to cut through to the truth with an acid tongue. Joni had no difficulty in letting someone know how disappointed she was in their actions. At the tender age of sixteen, she seemed wise beyond her years. This second reading was no different. She spent a large part of the reading chastising her older sister for the choices she had repeatedly made and continued to make following Joni's death.

Joni does not leave much for people to interpret in her messages. She was very straightforward in life and had not changed following her physical death. Joni told her sister that although she loved her nephew beyond words, her nephew's father was a waste of life. She could not understand why her sister would repeatedly go back to a man who would not step up and support his son. Joni made it quite clear that he was interested in one thing and one thing only. She stated that since her death, she knew her sister had gone back to this man twice, and it had to stop.

The look on her older sister's face was one of shock. Jodie referred to this man as a "pig with a penis." The laughter exploded in the room, and Dianne said "Oh my God, that is Joni; she always hated him!" Following this reading, I felt Joni's family would be able to start the healing process.

Five months passed before I heard from Dianne again. In late January 2003, I received a call requesting another reading. My first response was to refuse the request. I was constantly telling my clients they needed to deal with the issue of loss in their own way. Although what I did could have an undeniable healing effect on surviving family members, it in no way was a cure for grief on its own. I wanted and expected people to put the effort into their own lives and not to rely on me as a direct telephone line to the dead. Against my better judgment, I allowed Dianne to make the appointment. The date came and went, and Dianne never showed. Feelings of anger flowed. I felt that a phone call was warranted at the very least, as a consideration to me.

A couple more weeks passed, and after not hearing from Dianne I decided to call to make sure everything was okay. Dianne apologized for not keeping the appointment, explaining how bad the situation was that she was going through. I was still annoyed that a phone call had not been made, however just as in the first phone call, my heart went out to her. Another appointment was made, and this time it was delayed by two weeks due to the sudden death of Dianne's father. How much more could this poor woman endure?

We met a few weeks later even though I was apprehensive. I am not comfortable having someone become dependent on my ability, and I work hard to ensure this does not occur. Dianne had a hold on me, and I truly wanted to help her. Before our third reading, I asked Joni to please give me the messages that her mother needed to hear in order to start her healing.

When the day came for Dianne's reading, on my way to the office, Joni appeared in the car and asked me to play song seven from Celine Dion's CD *A New Day Has Come.*

I couldn't help but think this particular reading would be different. I believed Joni would do what it took to help her mother, and now having her grandfather with her, they would both surely do their best to help Dianne.

The reading started with the older male coming through first. "I have a male with a 'G' name coming through; who is Greg?" I asked.

Tears flowed freely as Dianne said, "That's my father."

We were off and running.

He wanted Dianne to know he was with Joni and that he was very happy and very lucky to be with her. Greg continued to talk about his health issues and his passing.

Although Dianne wanted to hear from her dad, it was obvious she needed to hear from Joni, and she didn't have long to wait. Joni stood next to her mother and, with a tone in her voice that I had not heard before, she told her mother she needed to do her part in healing. Joni talked about her older sister and the fact that Dianne had had a falling out with her. They needed to reconnect, and Joni stated very clearly that her sister needed to grow up and take responsibility for herself and her choices.

Dianne acknowledged that they had a falling out a couple months before and had not talked since.

Joni also told her mother that she thought they would be selling their family business and that she needed to take the time this would afford her to reconnect the family. Once again, Dianne laughed and said that she and her husband, Daniel, were considering selling their company.

Throughout Dianne's reading Joni made it very clear that Dianne was failing when it came to life. She told her mother that she was not doing one thing well. Speaking plainly, she said that Dianne was letting herself, Joni's siblings and Joni down. She pleaded for her mother to take a stand and start the healing process.

Joni's messages were very stern in nature, and I was uncomfortable in giving them to Dianne. I was afraid that Joni's words and my style of delivery would push Dianne over the edge, but I had asked Joni to come through and make a difference for her mother. I now had to trust that she knew what she was doing. It was a role reversal unlike anything else I had ever witnessed; Joni was playing the part of the parent, using tough love to get Dianne to see the possible errors of her ways.

When the reading was nearing an end, Joni reminded me of her request. I told Dianne that Joni had asked me to play a song for her. A song that would let her mother know what she means to her.

I played "Good-bye" for Dianne. I sat next to her for comfort, and I could feel Joni's presence and knew she was saying good-bye for now to her mother. The tears washed down Dianne's face, and I could only pray that Dianne was feeling what I knew was taking place. A daughter so loved her mother that she found the perfect song, the perfect words to tell her mother what she meant to her.

In closing Joni's story, I would like to leave you with the last few lines from "Good-bye."

> *Someday you'll say that word and I will cry*
> *It'll break my heart to hear you say good-bye*
> *Till we meet again until then good-bye.*

MADD Medium

I was unaware of it at the time, but the client I was about to meet would change my professional life and would be responsible for assisting me with being the first medium in the country to work with MADD Canada.

My client, Pat, walked into my office late one July afternoon. A warm smile greeted me when I stood up to meet her. She was a well-dressed lady who at first glance seemed incredibly controlled and self-confident.

After some short pleasantries, we were ready to begin. I felt the presence of an older person first, followed quickly by the undeniable presence of a young man. I learned Tim was his name, and he waited patiently to talk to his mother. He began by talking of being in two places when it came to health care. He showed me the image of a car wreck and the fact that he did not pass immediately. Tim gave the numbers of sixteen and twenty-one, and without any change in her facial expression, Pat acknowledged what she heard.

Tim took full responsibility for his actions and apologized for the hurt this brought to his family and others. The smell of alcohol came strong with his next message, and I relayed what he was showing me. His mother simply nodded and said, "We assumed so."

His heartfelt thanks came as waves of strong energy sweeping over me. I conveyed to his mother how appreciative he was of all she had done for him. If the ability of mediumship has one downfall, this was it: the incredible emotions and heartfelt thanks that our loved ones try to express somehow fall into a void as I try to show the sincere love they are letting me glimpse as they say thanks. When this occurs, I will get a sweeping feeling that encases my entire body making goose bumps and the hair on my arms stand straight. No matter how I try verbally to pass this emotion on, I am afraid I fall short.

Tim spent over an hour with his mother that day, telling her things about his life as well as events that occurred following his physical death. He told her how proud he was of her ability to turn loss into education for others.

As the reading concluded, I remember thinking that was interesting but probably not very good for my client. Pat had sat through her reading in a very sombre state, not saying much and showing very little emotion. It was only once the reading was over that she felt she could talk. A veil had dropped.

She was in fact very happy with the reading and spent the next half hour filling me in on the details of what was said during her session.

Pat wrote the following after our afternoon together.

The time has come for me to put my thoughts into writing about my experience with Christopher Stillar. What a remarkable man! The time I spent with Chris during my reading was hard to describe, but I came away from it with feelings of great emotion. I went to him with a very open mind. My only hope with the outcome of my reading was to somehow make a connection with my son, Tim. The connection was truly made!

Chris first touched on Tim when he made mention of a person who had passed, who had been in two places, one being medical and one being home. Our son, Tim, was seriously injured in a car accident at the age of sixteen, and he became a quadriplegic, never to speak another word to us again.

He lived in this semi-comatose state for five and a half years before passing away. The accident happened in 1982, and Tim died on March 15, 1988. Tim spent time at Sunnybrook, Queen Elizabeth and Markdale hospitals before I made the decision to bring him home to be with his family again, to receive the quality of life I felt he deserved. It meant giving him care around the clock. This was mentioned in my reading, along with Tim being uncomfortable with some of the care that had to be provided to him. I could relate to this greatly, because Tim could do absolutely nothing for himself. I had to do everything for him, and that had to be humiliating for him.

Chris later mentioned that I used my grief to help others. I was awakened one night out of a sound sleep and told that I should travel with Tim to schools and do a presentation regarding drinking and driving. The next morning I phoned the school that Tim was to have attended, inquiring if I could bring Tim to their school and speak to the students about drinking and driving. The answer was yes. I hung up the phone thinking, What do I say? Within a half hour, I had written the words, and Tim and I made our debut. What a response we had!

Tim touched so many lives, even though he never spoke a word! You could hear a pin drop. I was later told that the students at this school had never been this quiet. Many tears fell, because many knew Tim and our family. This presentation snowballed, and we continued to do many presentations all over Ontario for the remaining year of Tim's life.

A video was made of our presentation, and my family was invited in the years after Tim's death to travel to many other schools with our message. When Tim was living and I did the presentation, I would never allow myself to focus on our closing song, because it broke my heart. After Tim died and I would do this presentation, I was deep into the closing song because it made me realize how very much I missed Tim, and all I had left of him was memories.

Throughout my reading with Chris, Tim came through to offer great thanks for all I had done for him when I cared for him, and that gave me such extreme comfort! Mention was also made of how I had to allot time for others, which was so true. I needed to spend time with Tim's dad, Keith, plus his siblings, Tammy and Jeremy.

Another point Tim made during my reading was his apology for the choice he made that caused his accident. We were never told, but strongly felt, that alcohol or drugs was a major factor in his car accident—truly a wrong choice on his part. He did apologize for that a few times. Chris asked me if I had written since Tim's accident, which surprised me when I heard it. Every day from the day of Tim's accident, until I brought him home again, I would write a daily journal to help me cope with the dramatic changes in our family. Some days I would write as many as seven pages because of what had happened that day. Chris said he saw a hardcover book. My future plans included writing a book entitled *A Mother's Love: The Story of Tim Franks* to tell others of the many things we dealt with after Tim's accident, to possibly encourage other families that experience what we did. It takes an extreme amount of courage and strength to carry on, and I would hope to help others in any way that I can. I have attempted to start this book but have always been sidetracked. I often wondered if my family was really ready to read what I had to say. It is going to happen, and I know the time is near to begin this venture. I pray I have the strength to walk through it all again, inch by inch.

Chris mentioned in my reading about something high and something low in our home, even going so far as to say something is downstairs at the bottom of the steps, a table. I have an antique table with Tim's picture, along with a writing with a rose on the page that is so beautiful, entitled, "When I'm Gone." I have angels sitting among these things and a candle I received with a golden angel on it. It is a table in memory of my son Tim, and it is very special to me.

I cannot begin to sum up the great comfort I received from my reading with Chris, but to have the connection with Tim in so many meaningful ways was awesome, and I thank you, Chris, from the bottom of my heart.

Sincerely,
Pat Franks

MADD Comes Calling

Sometimes when you least expect something, that is when opportunity comes knocking. Such was the case one cold January morning when the mail signal went off on my computer. Once again some of the names in the following account have been changed.

The message sent to me was from a past client named Pat Franks, who was affiliated with MADD (Mothers Against Drunk Driving) Canada, asking me if I would be interested in hosting a seminar on Spirit Communication at MADD's Annual Victims Weekend and Vigil, coming up a few months later. After I read the e-mail for a second time, I realized this wasn't a joke and responded with a resounding yes.

I was ecstatic with the notion that a national organization was interested in having me come and conduct a seminar and demonstration at a national event. What better way to legitimize my work than to be recognized by such a well-known and valuable organization. It seemed almost too good to be true. Even though the e-mail was only asking if I was interested at this point, I knew I would be doing this and that it would go well. My guides, Grey Owl and Gabriel, were telling me this was what I had been waiting for. The e-mail was followed a couple of weeks later by a phone call from the Director of Victim Services of MADD Canada. The conversation was very memorable for a couple of reasons: I knew instinctively that this woman was not entirely open to this and that she didn't personally believe in what I claimed I could do. Despite this, I still believed I would carry out this mission; please make no mistake about it—a mission it was.

After a few questions from her, I said with a chuckle, "You are not at all comfortable with this, are you? What does your gut say you should do about this situation?"

Her response was quick and to the point: "My gut says to do it."

I understood the seriousness of what was taking place; I simply had a heads-up on the outcome because I was being shown by my guides that I would definitely be doing this event. I explained to her that those who would get messages were meant to and that I trusted they would gain great healing from their loved ones. I could understand that MADD was going out on a limb even proposing this. Never before had this been attempted, let alone brought forth as an option of grief therapy for their victims. To be honest, the fact that I would be the first medium ever to be invited and endorsed by this organization did not escape me. I suggested to her that I put aside an evening for up to twelve people of their choosing to come to my office. I would spend a few hours demonstrating just exactly what it is I did. The idea piqued her interest, and the following month a date was set for twelve people to venture into unknown territory.

One by one the small group arrived, and it was time to begin. Even at this point I was not nervous. I began the evening just like any other reading, explaining the preliminaries of a reading such as things like how to answer any questions asked, certain terminology that I use when trying to figure out the relationship of their loved ones, and the like.

Three hours, two dogs, a couple of children who were victims from drunk driving and a parent or two later, the evening was concluded. Those who received messages seemed very happy and delighted with what they heard. There was one exception in the group: one woman, whose grandfather came through many times with facts and details about his life and hers, was not able to accept publicly what I knew she knew privately. I had heard after the fact that what I said to her was very accurate, but she was still not prepared to come to terms with it yet.

A few days later it was confirmed that I was included in the weekend's events. The weekend arrived, and I awoke early that morning in the hotel room filled with excitement. I was ready to get started.

My seminar was to start at 9:00 a.m. but by 8:45 the conference room was filled, and we started fifteen minutes early. After being introduced by one of the MADD representatives, I began. Never knowing what topics and personal knowledge or lack thereof will flow out of my mouth, I have learned to trust that I will say what needs to be said. Faith is a wonderful thing.

Some of the organizers were not sure what to expect, and they were ready for the worst. To their credit, MADD had professional people waiting outside the conference room, ready to handle anyone who found the seminar too emotional. I am happy to write that not one person found the need to leave. Laughter was obviously the order for the day. Those in spirit who came through that day used humour to put people at ease and to heal the pain of loss. One family's daughter, Catherine, came through from spirit acknowledging that their family used to laugh about an older female who suffered from dementia. The Newton family connected this to an earlier mention of a candy dish and validated their daughter's statement, which was an inside family joke. Catherine even went on to tease the family's youngest daughter, who was in attendance that day, for being messy. "Your sister is showing me the vanity counter in the bathroom being heaped with makeup and stuff." The second sister in attendance said, "Oh my God, I just said that exact thing to her this morning in the hotel; I actually told her she was a pig." The audience screamed with laughter.

One of the more touching aspects of that day wasn't fully realized by myself until a couple of days following the event. A letter arrived two days later from Helen St. Jacques. The following is the actual letter written to me:

Tuesday, April 29, 2003
Hi Chris.

My three daughters and I attended your seminar last Sunday at the MADD weekend. Kristen is my youngest daughter. If you remember, she was the first person you spoke to. I wanted to let you know that you have had a huge impact on her. It has only been a couple of days, but I have already seen a difference in her. Since her father was killed two years ago, she has been very bitter (as you told her) and withdrawn, has no interest in anything and has the attitude of, "Oh well, I don't really care about anything anyway." I have tried everything with her and could not break her out of her moods and depression. I have been very concerned about her.

Since your reading on Sunday, she has done a complete turnaround, and I feel that I have my youngest daughter back. She had her picture taken with you after the seminar, and I know she will cherish it. She hasn't stopped talking about you and the reading you gave her. My only regret is that when you kept asking for a name with an ST, I didn't bite. My last name is St. Jacques. I was so shocked about the reading you gave Kristen and the fact that you spent so much time talking to her that I didn't want to say anything in case it wasn't for me. I guess I didn't want too much focus on my family, and I didn't want to take away from anyone else, but that is okay because if Kristen has her way; she will see you again in the future, I am sure.

Once again, thank you.
Helen

I have to give credit to the MADD organization, and specifically to Pat Franks, for starting the ball rolling. I also have to thank Ardene Vicioso, a wonderful woman who has always stuck her neck out for this guy who said he could talk to the dead and who has believed in him. To all my many friends I have made over the years at MADD Canada, thank you.

My soul is strengthened to see that many people have put their lives back together and not only cope after a child's passing but actually start to live again. To all those parents who have suffered the loss of a child, I pray that you will find the strength, the energy and the purpose to carry on—to not only carry on, but to excel at whatever your life's calling is. It certainly won't be easy, but I have seen it done countless times by parents that find purpose in their remaining days. No one has the right to tell you how to feel, or how you should act as a result of your loss. I simply want you to know there are people who understand.

For all who have lost children, my wish is that you all discover the truth that your children are still with you—and yes, they still talk to you. My question for all of you is this: Are you listening?

Chapter 15
EXPECT THE UNEXPECTED

"I never would have thought" is a very common phrase that I hear repeatedly when I am conducting a session. So many times people come to a medium with a one-track mind. They decide ahead of time on the one or two people from which they want to hear. Perhaps it is a sister, a parent or even their children they most want to contact. These thoughts are fine as long as they realize there are many people from their past in spirit, and it is not up to them or the medium to decide who will communicate.

Often people are looking for proof of life after death, and this is a good thing. However, do not determine ahead of time what that proof will be, because you will only set yourself up for disappointment. Thinking "Mom must have a message" does not make it so. Many times the spirit who is expected comes through, but sometimes he or she doesn't. Remember that whoever does come through has an important message. The most startling, earth-shattering results can come from someone in spirit we would never have thought of. The following two stories are examples of this.

Jim Berry

Ev Berry is a retired schoolteacher with more than three successful decades of teaching, inspiring and molding the young minds of yesterday and today. Ev is a curious woman when it comes to psychic phenomena, spiritual issues and the possibility of life after death. She is far from gullible, balancing her beliefs with a healthy skepticism. This particular day would put to rest any of her uncertainties about life after death. The visit was our second meeting; a year earlier she had come to a private consultation I did for her two daughters.

CHRIS   *Someone is giving me the letters BER. Do they mean anything to you?*

EV   *They are the first three letters of my last name.*

I had no idea what her surname name was; as was the custom with all my bookings, I took first names only and a phone number in case I should have to reschedule.

CHRIS   *Standing before me is a large man. He is very broad and seems fairly tall. His hair is brushed up and off his forehead. Think in terms of a football player.*

Ev sat intently listening and trying to piece together this new puzzle that seemed to be scattered in front of her. She said nothing.

CHRIS   *This man is telling me that his name is Jim. "J" is the first letter, and I am sure he's saying Jim. He tells me he died from a heart attack, very quickly.*

EV   *That is my husband's name. Even the description fits my husband.*

CHRIS   *Okay, but your husband isn't deceased, is he? It has to be somebody else. Even as I'm seeing this, I have no idea what is happening. I know what this man's telling me, so we must be missing something. Jim's telling me he had a massive heat attack. He drops suddenly and hits something on the way down. He is also saying he was in a public place when he died. I really don't know where—it might be a bar, I'm not sure, but it is definitely a public place.*

Ev sat trying to see how this information could possibly fit. Nothing seemed to match up or make sense to her. I could see that she was feeling somewhat frustrated.

CHRIS   *Jim's saying the word teacher, teacher over and over. Did your husband teach as a profession, too?*

EV   *No, he didn't … Oh my God! It's Jim Berry!*

Now I was more confused than ever. Ev was all smiles as she explained to me that Jim was the principal at the school where she had last taught.

EV   *He hasn't been dead a year yet. His name was Jim Berry, too—he had the same name as my husband.*

A warm feeling came over me; we knew who this man was. Ev continued telling me that Jim had been working out on the treadmill at a public gym. He was struck by a fatal heart attack and collapsed. Jim was very pleased that Ev remembered him.

CHRIS   *He is thanking you for all you have done for him. He explains that he implemented new policies or procedures within the school that were not always well-received. You supported him, and he says thanks.*

Now Jim turned the reading into a test for Ev.

CHRIS   *He is asking you to do him a favour. I'm not sure how you will do this, or even if you will, but he is asking it of you over and over. He says, "Please tell my wife that I am fine, I am doing okay and I haven't gone anywhere."*

When I glanced over at Ev and waited for a response, I saw that she didn't know what to say. Her mouth hung open, and she was searching for words. Before she could say anything, I told her that I knew this was a hard thing to do, but Jim needed her help. Could she find it in herself to help him?

CHRIS   *I don't know how you will find the strength or the way to deliver his message, Ev, but I know you have to try. He's saying please; his wife is having a hard time accepting this. She needs to know he is okay.*

Ev assured me that even though she didn't know Jim's wife well, she would invite her out for coffee and somehow find a way to relay the message.

I find it astounding how those in the spirit world find ways of achieving their desired outcomes. Obviously Jim's wife was having a hard time coping with the loss of her husband, and maybe, just maybe getting a message from a casual acquaintance would help her to move forward with her life.

Ev Berry followed up on Jim's request and wrote me a letter telling me what took place. I have included Ev's letter verbatim.

Dear Chris,

Thank you for accepting the invitation to do a spiritual enlightenment with my two daughters, Gladys and Gloria; three of my granddaughters, Nicole, Sherry and Cheryl; and myself.

This has changed my perception of life after death and how beautiful Heaven must be was relayed in your session that day. I came to the meeting with an open mind—whoever came through with a message for anyone of my family members would be just great. I was astonished when you said, "Ev, this message is for you."

Chris, you first started saying J, then Jim twice—how this spirit described himself in such great detail of how he looked, what kind of a person he was and how he was connected with teaching. He then proceeded to thank me twice for being so supportive of him when I worked for him, teaching school for three years. He continued to tell how he had died and that his wife, Penny, was having a hard time trying to deal with this. He wanted me to relay the message that he was around his wife trying to help her. His message to her was that he was okay.

I could not believe that a spirit would come through in such great detail. By the end of the session, Chris, you had me fully convinced that it was my duty to somehow fill his request.

Not knowing his wife very well, I decided to retape the message you had relayed to me. I phoned Penny, and we set up a time and place to meet. I made no indication to Penny why I was inviting her to the coffee shop.

I spent most of the night before tossing and turning, trying to decide how I would break the ice with her. I wondered if she would ask why he had chosen me. I decided he had worked with me for three years and knew me well enough to know when a job was to be done, I'd do it. After him thanking me twice for being so supportive, I felt I owed it to him.

I drove to Orangeville and arrived at the coffee shop ten minutes early to prepare myself. I chose a table in the corner. Time passed, and we conversed about different people and events. Finally I decided now was the time. I looked at Penny and said, "I had an experience that I would like to share with you."

I asked her if she believed in spirits, angels and psychic work. I asked her if she knew what a medium was. Then I proceeded to tell her I had been to one of these meetings, and a very special message came through that I believed was for her. I began to explain how he described himself, his teaching, his death and her.

As I continued to explain, she nodded and tears came several times. The more I unloaded, the more convinced she appeared to be. It was hard to know at times who was having more difficulty holding back the tears.

Finally I decided she had heard all she could handle. I told her that I had made a tape for her, and I would like her to have it. I apologized if I had upset her in any way. We went to my car and I gave her the tape. She hugged me, thanked me and said she realized this must have been very hard for me to do.

As I left I felt upset but relieved. That night I went to bed with a weight lifted from my shoulders that had been hanging heavy since I first realized I had this job to do.

Later when I talked to Penny, she told me she came home and cried all day. It seemed so real that she had the impression Jim was talking to her. She felt good that their relationship had meant so much to him.

I gave her a book called Signals *to read about other people who had received messages and their experiences. Penny said later she knew Jim was coming to her that night. She prayed it would not be a frightening experience. She felt him sit on the side of the bed, and then he put his arms around her.*

Before this spiritual experience, I had been skeptical about life after death. From the detailed messages that came through from Jim, my sister Muriel and my mother, there is no doubt now that when death comes, we leave our physical bodies behind, and our spirits travel to

Heaven. I believe at times they have messages for us and that they choose how to relay those messages. I also believe that the major events in our lives have been planned well ahead by God.

Chris, you must be a very special person that God has chosen to be able to channel these important messages to us in such great detail.

God bless you.
Ev Berry

Coming Back to Say Thank You

Sometimes readings can turn on a dime. Even though I am a medium, I never know who will choose to communicate or what direction the reading will take. Such was the case with this next story. The first forty-five minutes of the session were fairly typical. Marge's grandfather had come through and talked extensively of her life, her choices and what lay ahead for her. It was the person who came through next that would first cause confusion and ultimately a warm, loving reunion.

Standing next to Marge was a beautiful woman from spirit who entered with confidence, enveloped in a warm and loving glow. This woman's love radiated out toward the two of us. She had been extremely patient waiting her turn, and now it was time.

I saw her as a short lady with a large body, top and bottom. Her dark hair had little gray streaks that darted through it. When she spoke, her Eastern Canadian accent was very apparent.

To Marge, this was all very confusing, and none of it seemed to make sense. As this wonderful lady came closer, she said, "My name is Rita. Tell her I'm Rita."

The name had no impact on Marge.

Rita described suffering from emphysema in the last months of her life. She told me her lungs had hardened and eventually stopped working. I related all this to Marge, but still nothing registered for her or myself. We both struggled for answers.

"Rita is instructing me to tell you that she was a friend, not a relative. She is also showing me a school bus."

I could see a look of frustration on Marge's face. Rita's joy had turned to sorrow that Marge did not remember her, but she tried one more time." She is thanking you over and over. She says you helped her cope with the loss of a loved one. It was not a child she lost, it was someone older."

Just as I finished relaying Rita's message, I could see the light come on inside Marge. She gave me a look of astonishment and sighed. Rita had gone from sadness back to the happy, bubbly person she was when she came in. I knew we had a breakthrough.

With a smile, Marge told me of the connection she shared with Rita. "Yes, yes ... You even had her name and everything, and I did not remember her. Rita was just about the nicest lady I ever met. She was part of a grief-counselling group I was instructing a few years back. Her husband had passed from an aneurysm. He had been a bus driver up until his death. I remember Rita telling me she was so thankful that her husband had the aneurysm while he was in the garage preparing for his daily bus run, and not driving with a bus full of children. That's just the way Rita was: even in her darkest moments of loss, she was able to find a reason to give thanks. And yes, she definitely was from the East Coast. I also remember the depth of her grief because she was so close to her husband; they never had any children."

"Rita wants you to know how thankful she is for what you did for her, Marge. She is very pleased that you remember her."

"You're so very welcome, my friend," said Marge, and then Rita laughed and was gone.

It is my hope that these two examples will show how the unexpected can and does take place during a psychic reading. So remember, when visiting a medium, one should never have expectations for who may or may not come through to talk. It is always best to have a clear mind and an open heart when sitting with a medium.

Chapter 16
GREY OWL AND GABRIEL SPEAK

For the final chapter, I felt it right and appropriate to let the spirit world have the last say. I asked my guides to respond to several topics of interest, and this is what they said. Here are their messages.

Life

"A flower and a clock are symbolic of life: they are the essence of physical life. We are all flowers that are growing. We begin as seedlings or bulbs, and we grow and reach up. While we do this, there is a clock ticking away next to us. We concentrate so much on time: I am running late, I don't have enough time to play with the kids, I am going to be late for work. Whatever it may be, we would do well to throw away the clocks and stop timing ourselves." Grey Owl points directly at me for this, and I realize I put too many time limits on myself.

"It is not enough for us that we are perfect beings growing and reaching like the tiny flower; we have to have the clock for everything we do. The old saying that time is our enemy is only true because we have made it that way. Have you ever noticed the people that seem unaffected by time? They march to the beat of their own drum. Time is never a reflection of who they are. If they are late, oh well; perhaps they are always late. Notice the freedom, the carefree attitude by which they live. These people have mastered the concept of time. There will always be enough because time doesn't exist."

Parenting

"The most important act we perform in the physical sense is parenting, the raising of young children and the filling of young minds. With every tiny birth we are given a new beginning. If we choose as a society not to nurture that tiny flower, that tiny bulb, we are destined to repeat the ways of our past. Do not think that experience is your best teacher; this is only true if you remember past lessons. To repeat over and over is not to step forward. Advancement comes only when we remember and stop repeating.

"Look back and see where you have come from, but keep your primary focus ahead of you. Where do you choose to go from here? We seem to learn in the physical sense through experience, and we raise our children as our parents raised us. If we were raised in a negative environment, and we have the strength and willpower to break the cycle, sometimes we do the complete opposite, and that is great. For the most part, however, we repeat what we know.

I would encourage all of you to reach out and to dream larger than your parents did for you. In doing so, light the path for the children of today and tomorrow so they too can create their own futures. As parents, you should be safety bumpers for them to bounce off of, so no harm comes to them. The path should be free for them to take. Gently guide them while giving them the freedom we all crave."

Helping Others

How is it best for us to teach people, to show people, to freely give to people so that they might discover their own truth? Grey Owl draws in close, puts his hands on my shoulders, bends down to my right ear and whispers, "By example."

Grey Owl's energy is coursing through me at this moment. "What better way to light the path than to be a light. You cannot expect people to be more direct, open and truthful than you are. You cannot expect people to be more honest and loving than you are. Walk your path, walk it straight and walk it with confidence. Walk it with knowing and with faith, and no brighter light shall ever shine on the path of true love."

Judgment

"Never has there been a bigger stumbling block than judgment. Never has there been a bigger learning tool, a tool to self-discovery. A two-year-old toddler keeps walking up to a big block. He's not able to crawl over it; instead he keeps running into it and stubbing his toe. Once, twice, three times—finally on the tenth time, he realizes he is hurting his toe. He steps back, takes a look and notices there is a path around the block to the right and he takes it. The block represents a judgment; we are the toddler. How many times do we need to stub our toes before we realize there is a path around?"

"Is judgement bad?" I ask.

Grey Owl laughs because he knows good and bad are relative. "If your perspective is that stubbing your toe ten times is bad, then it is bad, but if in the process of stubbing your toe you prevent the eleventh stubbing and you realize you can walk around, is that not good?"

I invite you all to study these simple words. Do they not ring with truth? Life does not have to be complex, difficult or frustrating—unless we choose it to be.

Choices, Opportunities and Perspective

"Two young boys grow up in the same environment with very little money and few family values. What makes one child go on and flourish while the other struggles and barely gets by? One excels in his personal life—academically, professionally, financially and spiritually—and also has a wonderful, loving family. The other is pulled along by the events of life. The answer, which has been given many times, is choice. The first boy stubbed his toe then walked around. The second boy continues to stub his toe. It is all about our perspective on life, on the events that happen and how we view them and handle them.

Souls That Seem Lost

"Grey Owl, what of the people who feel desolate and think they cannot go on?" I ask. "Everything said to them falls on deaf ears. How can we help people like that?"

"It has already been answered, by example. Live your life as a bright light; where light is, darkness cannot exist. Your job, your goal is not to help these people. Your goal is to allow them to live their lives as bright as they can. If by your example, those in need see a path that has been lit for them, that is wonderful, but it must be by their own choosing, their decision, their perspective that they come out of the darkness and into the light."

Good Help vs. Bad Help

"'Good help' helps others become self-sufficient. It shows them the tools that exist inside themselves, tools that enable them to become the person they want to be through personal choice. 'Bad help' is making or allowing someone to be dependent on us—whether that person sees us as spiritual gurus and hangs on to our every word, or we always come up with financial aid for someone who does not know how to manage money; this allows one to be dependent on another. This is not 'good help.'

"The goal of parents is to help every child become self-sufficient, so that when the parents' physical death occurs, the child is able to go on with his or her own life and function independently. Too many bright lights are diminished by dependence on others. Please remember there are many, many, many paths to righteousness and to one's truth."

Truth

"Truth comes in many forms, from many directions and in many ways. Each of us must discover our own truth. There is no right or wrong; there is only one's truth."

Death

I asked the question, "What of death? Does everyone experience the same process or steps with death and what follows physical death?"

Gabriel answered, "There are many roads to eternity; for every soul there is a path so unique, so individual in design that the answer to your question is no, not everyone experiences the same steps and processes. We are individuals, we are connected to the same light, we have the same source in the centre of each of us—yet we have different paths for getting back to that source, and that is as it should be."

I asked, "But do we experience similar steps? Is the talk of the light and the tunnel true for everyone?"

"Only if we choose it to be. Inspiration! Inspiration!"

"What do you mean by inspiration, Gabriel?"

"We have total control over the death process. The one thing that is common and yet unique is that we are never alone. We always have friends with us. We have loving energies that surround us and inspire us. These energies are also known as family. You are never alone during this process. How you choose to come through it is totally up to you. We are the greatest individual creators of all time. Why would you stop creating at the point known as physical death? Some people create consciously, and some people create unconsciously; so it is with the process of change. I encourage everyone to create consciously, to make choices consciously. There is always love waiting for us just as on earth. There is always love around us, even if we choose not to see it or feel it.

"Death is nothing more than the opening up of truth. If you come to the truth while in the physical life, death is much less of a process to go through. Should you not remember this while in the physical life, death may take a bit longer to adjust to, but as soon as you choose consciously, so shall it be. Should you choose to see a tunnel, you will; should you choose to see loved ones, you will; should you choose to feel lost, you will. No matter the choice, it will last only as long as you choose to experience it."

Coping with a Loss

There is no right or wrong. We are all individuals and we all have choices. If you knew the outcome ahead of time; if you knew your child, your parent, your sister or your spouse was in a happier and better place; if you knew they were still around you and you could still see and feel them—would you mourn as deeply? I think not. I promise you your loved ones go on and is around you now even as you read this. He or she loved you and continues to love you. Spend time with yourself in moments of stress and sorrow. Reflect on your truth; it resides within you at all times. We are energy, and energy can change but cannot be destroyed. We cannot see air; even when it is in motion, we can only feel it. The same is true of the energy of our loved ones. When they move about, you can feel them. We must become aware of the subtle changes of energy that are constantly moving all around us.

Take as long as you need for sorrow; missing someone is a great heartbreak, but remember, your loved ones have not really gone. They stand next to you with their hands on your shoulders to support you. They kiss your cheek in times of sorrow, and they laugh out loud in the moments that you are the happiest. Open yourself up to them.

In Closing ...

All things must come to an end—at least, that is how the saying goes. I hope I have been able to demonstrate, through this book and the incredible true stories of survival following physical death, that not all things do end. Life is a continuous cycle and does go on forever. It is my desire that you take away the fact that your loved ones who have taken their final journeys to the Other Side are still a very real and vital part of your daily lives. They see, hear and feel what is taking place in the physical world. I convey this concept to my clients daily, reassuring them that their loved ones in spirit are aware of their thoughts and feelings even before they are spoken. So take the time to say hello each and every day when you are missing that special someone. There truly is no reason to feel you ever need to say good-bye to those you love.

I want to thank you for being a part of my journey. I have been extremely blessed in my lifetime and have discovered just how rich my life is, and it is my wish for you all that you find your own pennies from Heaven.

CPSIA information can be obtained
at www.ICGtesting.com
Printed in the USA
LVHW02s1951190118
563180LV00002B/5/P